ce

The Collected Poems of

# EDWARD THOMAS

# The Collected Poems of
# EDWARD THOMAS

*Edited by*
R. GEORGE THOMAS

Oxford New York
OXFORD UNIVERSITY PRESS

Oxford University Press, Walton Street, Oxford OX2 6DP

London Glasgow New York Toronto
Delhi Bombay Calcutta Madras Karachi
Kuala Lumpur Singapore Hong Kong Tokyo
Nairobi Dar es Salaam Cape Town
Melbourne Auckland

and associate companies in
Beirut Berlin Ibadan Mexico City Nicosia
OXFORD is a trade mark of Oxford University Press

This edition is based on The Collected Poems of Edward Thomas,
Oxford University Press, 1978. First issued, with a new introduction,
as an Oxford University Press paperback, 1981.

Reprinted 1983

British Library Cataloguing in Publication Data

Thomas, Edward, b. 1878
The collected poems of Edward Thomas.
I. Thomas, Richard George
821'.9'12  PR6039.H55A17  80–49864
ISBN 0–19–281288–2

Printed in Great Britain by
J. W. Arrowsmith Ltd
Bristol

# CONTENTS

# CONTENTS

# CONTENTS

## 1916

# CONTENTS

# INTRODUCTION

## I

THIS edition of *The Collected Poems of Edward Thomas* is an attempt to present the poems in chronological order, as closely as possibly to the form in which they would have appeared if Thomas had seen them through the press in 1917. He in fact saw few of his poems in print, and not all of those had the benefit of his well-trained proof-reader's eye. The detailed evidence of his notebooks, manuscripts and typescripts is fully documented in my textual edition of *The Collected Poems* (Clarendon Press, 1978), together with a selection of variant readings, early drafts and prose versions. The text of the 144 poems printed here is taken from that edition.*

In this form, one hopes, the lover of poetry will be able to recognize the intensity and the frustrations with which an accomplished prose writer and esteemed literary critic came to terms with the discovery that, through the medium of verse, he could best uncover the hidden depths of his own nature in 'a language not to be betrayed'. The uneven quality of some of his verse reflects the fierce honesty with which he sought to uncover the doubts as well as the certainties within his own make-up. The tenacious craftsmanship that marks his prior eighteen years as a writer of prose is revealed in the flexibility of his exploration of this new medium of expression. His best poems have a resonance that nowadays—over sixty years after his death—finds echoes among a growing body of readers from all walks of life and of widely differing age-groups. I believe he would have readily understood the slow growth of his reputation which began to accelerate almost half a century after his death. One character in his 'A Colloquy in a Library' (1900) asserts that 'it is true that I live, as Leonardo wrote, backwards; but even were it otherwise, I should be like one bereft of memory or her keys, without [books], and life would be more histrionic than ever'. Seventeen years later, in France, he wrote that his life as a front-line

---

*The printer's typescript of *Poems* (1917) by 'Edward Eastaway' has been made available since this volume went to press. Corrections in Thomas's own hand may suggest a few alterations to titles adopted for the Clarendon Press edition.

artillery officer was teaching him the worth of 'simple, primitive' things: a statement that runs parallel to his praise of

> . . . the small brown birds
> Wisely reiterating endlessly
> What no man learnt yet, in or out of school.

A consistency of purpose runs throughout Edward Thomas's writing life when he recalls moments of experience that he believed to be common to all human beings. Characteristically he gave expression to one such moment of insight in the final, tacked-on paragraph of a *Daily Chronicle* review in August 1908:

'But because we are imperfectly versed in history, we are not therefore blind to the past. The eye that sees the things of today, and the ear that hears, the mind that contemplates or dreams, is itself an instrument of antiquity equal to whatever it is called upon to apprehend. We are not merely twentieth-century Londoners or Kentish men or Welshmen. We belong to the days of Wordsworth, of Elizabeth, of Richard Plantagenet, of Harold, of the earliest bards. We, too, like Taliesin, have borne a banner before Alexander, have been with our Lord in the manger of the ass, have been in India, and with the "remnant of Troia", and with Noah in the ark, and our original country is "the region of the summer stars". And of these many folds in our nature the face of the earth reminds us, and perhaps even where there are no more marks visible upon the land than there were in Eden, we are aware of the passing of time in ways too difficult and strange for the explanation of historian and zoologist and philosopher. It is the manifold nature that responds with such indescribable depth and variety to the appeals of many landscapes.'

This sense of oneness with man in his natural surroundings is the nub of his enduring appeal to late twentieth-century readers.

From 1903 onwards, Edward Thomas had included many passages in his widely varied prose books which he charged with a particular intensity and which he, and his friends, called prose-poems. These insets, like his finest poems, are representative of his own sifted response to experience and bear reference to a wider world than his somewhat restricted life. They are about Steep, about Wales, about numerous London commons and Wiltshire canals, about the long-lived-in Heart of England, about the lost ideal world we are all reluctant to abandon. As Walter de la Mare divined in his Foreword to the first *Collected Poems* (1920), this poetry is personal to an intense degree: but in recent years it has become a publicly treasured possession. At its best, with ironic self-pity but without self-absorption, it remains a veiled, undeniable act of self-discovery, and also a remarkable response to war.

## II

Philip Edward Thomas was born in London on 3 March 1878. His parents were Londoners, born in Wales, and his father was a civil servant who had begun life in Tredegar as a schoolteacher. Edward was the eldest of six sons, and as the family grew he spent his childhood successively in Lambeth, Wandsworth, Clapham, and, finally, in Balham. After an ordinary childhood, marked by a strong interest in nature, he entered St. Paul's School, where he was a pupil for just over a year. During this time he was a frequent visitor to the home of the critic James Ashcroft Noble, who encouraged him to send his descriptions of nature to the weeklies. Edward followed his advice, and several articles were accepted for publication. It was also at this time that he began his friendship with Helen Noble, who was to become his wife. Edward eventually matriculated in 1897 as a non-collegiate student at Oxford and gaining a history scholarship to Lincoln College the next year, he studied under Owen M. Edwards. Throughout his career at Oxford he continued to publish his journalistic articles and earned about £80 a year. In June 1899 he and Helen were married in a London registry office, and just over a year later he graduated from Oxford with a second-class honours degree. He disappointed his father by refusing to enter the civil service, and decided to become a writer.

Edward's first years as a writer, a husband, and a father were not easy. A son, Merfyn, was born in 1900, and a daughter, Bronwen, in 1902. The family was badly off, and Edward had to sell many of his fine Oxford books to pay the bills. Shortly after his daughter's birth, however, he secured regular employment as Lionel Johnson's successor as a literary reviewer for *The Daily Chronicle*. Edward and Helen had decided to live in the country, but Edward found it necessary throughout his life to pay frequent visits to London in order to find work. Successively they moved house from Maidstone and the Weald, until they settled close to Bedales School in the district around Petersfield in December 1906. There his son and daughter were educated, while Helen regularly supplemented his income by teaching in the kindergarten and by accepting school boarders in the vacations; there, too, their second daughter, Myfanwy, was born. Edward Thomas lived in the Steep district until October 1916, first at Berryfield Cottage, then at a new house up on Wick Green (not far from his sarsen memorial stone) and, later, in the much smaller Yew Tree Cottage in the village. This corner of Hampshire provides the groundbass to the majority of his poems.

Between 1903 and September 1911 Thomas became a moderately successful reviewer, biographer, and topographical writer: he reviewed for *The Saturday Review*, *The Bookman*, and *The Morning Post*, as well as *The Daily Chronicle* and wrote his biography of Richard Jefferies and *The Heart of England*. He combined his strenuous life at Steep with frequent trips to London literary circles, walking tours in search of material for his nature books (and gradually for his own uncommissioned essays), and visits to Wales, Cornwall, and Cartmel. In his student days Thomas had suffered from bouts of depression, and as he grew older they recurred with debilitating regularity. He visited a variety of doctors, on whose advice he imposed a series of dietary regimes on himself and his family, but with little success. By the year 1911 his nervous exhaustion took the form of despair and sorely tried the spirit and cheerful support of his wife. He left home frequently, and a longish period in West Wales in the autumn of 1911—where he wrote *George Borrow*—did not bring, as often before, a tolerable return to his usual state of health. By this time, too, his regular sources of income had decreased, although his annual income remained roughly the same. He felt the need to leave his house for a smaller one in the village of Steep. Thereafter, until October 1914, his restlessness manifested itself in trips round the country, especially in Wiltshire and Somerset, and visits to friends like Clifford Bax and Vivian Locke Ellis, often as a paying guest. He also made two important new friends: Eleanor Farjeon, who became a devoted friend and a ready critic of his poetry, and the American poet Robert Frost, without whose encouragement Thomas might never have attempted to write verse. Throughout this difficult period Thomas began a fresh search for future subjects to place before shying publishers. He explored his own childhood memories remorselessly and ceaselessly, both in autobiographical and fictional form. Eventually, at Frost's prompting, he began to write verse that was based on some of his earlier prose descriptions of natural scenes and journeys. This was the beginning of his prolific, but short-lived career as a poet.

In August 1914, when Thomas had established his reputation as a significant critic of the new Georgian poetry, the war seemed to cut off all hope of his earning a living as a writer. There followed a period of vacillation and hard work—assisted by a grant from the Literary Fund—in which he sought posts as a teacher, a wartime historian or civil servant, toyed with the idea of emigrating to America with Frost, and finally enlisted in the Artists' Rifles in July 1915. He spent some months as a map-reading instructor at Hare Hall camp, was eventually commissioned as a 2/Lt. and posted to 244 Siege Battery, Royal Garrison Artillery in November 1916. In December he volunteered for service overseas and embarked for France on 29 January 1917. Despite the offer of alternative employment at Headquarters, he remained with his battery and was killed at the advanced Observation Post by a blast from a shell in the early bombardment of the Battle of Arras at 7.36 a.m. on Easter Monday, 9 April 1917.

Throughout his twenty years as an active writer, Edward Thomas's work reveals a remarkable degree of uniformity in subject matter and content. Unsure of himself in pursuing practical day-by-day aims and purposes, he contrived to preserve intact the inner core of his creed and practice as a writer. Frequently assailed by periods of depression from early manhood until his final pre-embarkation training in firing camp, and strongly imprisoned within an inherited Victorian compulsion to make adequate middle-class financial provision for his family, Thomas attempted at various times to enlarge the basis of his natural gifts as a writer in order to earn enough to pay his way and yet to preserve large tracts of free time in which he could write as he chose. He often accepted unworthy commissions. He engaged in multiple reviewing and the rapid production of many books, with the result that a few journalistic-critics, some of whom have never read much of his vast output, now thoughtlessly label him a 'hack-writer', a judgement which the unity of his letters, unpublished notebooks, articles, books, and reviews consistently refutes.

# III

Nothing can take away from Robert Frost the credit for pushing Edward Thomas into the writing of verse. In the spring of 1914 Frost pointed out to Thomas that much of the prose in his travel book *In Pursuit of Spring* (1914) was essentially the raw material of poetry. Thomas stated unequivocally in a letter that Frost was the 'onlie begetter' of his verse and Frost wrote privately in 1921 that 'there's a story going round that might lead you to exaggerate our debt to each other . . . I made him see that he owed it to himself and the poetry to have it out by himself in poetic form where it must suffer itself to be admired. . . The accent is absolutely his own. You can hear it everywhere in his prose, where if he had left it, however, it would have been lost.' This is a true record that matches everything we can know from those who saw the rapidly ripening friendship between the two writers between October 1913 when they first met and February 1915 when they last met at Steep before Frost sailed for America (with Merfyn, Edward's son). By this date Thomas had written his first thirty-three poems in three months. It was like the bursting of a long pent-up dam.

In February 1915 Edward was laid up with a damaged ankle but seemed determined to follow Robert Frost to New Hampshire and settle there as a farmer of sorts. His enlisting in July 1915 surprised his friends and family, but I doubt if Frost was correct in his belief that 'the decision he made in going into the army helped him make the other decision to be a poet in form'. The relationship between soldier and poet is typical of one side of Frost's own complex personality, but it is not the whole key to his friend's equally complex nature. From what I have seen of Edward Thomas's innumerable letters, his notebooks and the carefully preserved memoirs of his friends and relations, I would suggest, that after he had left Oxford in 1900 and decided to become a writer by profession, he never took a hasty decision on any practical matter until the need to act in response to an external demand coincided with a long maturing inner compulsion to act in the way he did. He was meticulous in his determination to support his family by his own efforts, in his acceptance of worthwhile writing commissions, in his judgement of books submitted to him for critical review, in the fierce self-control of his passionate nature. Equally, he tried to carry out these responsibilities without betraying his private conviction that the written word, intended for a worthy audience of whatever size, should match in sincerity the power of the experience a writer wished to convey. Few reviewers of his day were so acutely aware of the changing nature of the potential readership for good writing. When, some time in 1911, he appeared to have lost a suitably rewarding audience for his own personal kind of writing, he became even more introspective during a few years of severe self-examination in a manner that is conveyed later in the last section of his fourth poem, 'Old Man':

> I have mislaid the key. I sniff the spray
> And think of nothing; I see and I hear nothing;
> Yet seem, too, to be listening, lying in wait
> For what I should, yet never can, remember:
> No garden appears, no path, no hoar-green bush
> Of Lad's-love, or Old Man, no child beside,
> Neither father nor mother, nor any playmate;
> Only an avenue, dark, nameless, without end.

To read this daunting poem as either the sorry fruit of melancholy depression or an explicit account of an unhappy childhood is to falsify the available evidence of the poem's long gestation period and the quite different version of his childhood recorded in the autobiographical fragment *The Childhood of Edward Thomas*, or in the slightly fictionalized novel, *The Happy-Go-Lucky Morgans*. Both prose works belong to the thirty months of wandering and self-analysis that preceded Thomas's first meeting with Frost. During the same period he wrote two commissioned books, *Walter Pater, A Critical Study* and *In Pursuit of Spring*, which suggest that he was obsessively aware of the demand placed on a born writer to write 'living and social words':

'Only when a word has become necessary to him can a man use it safely; if he try to impress words by force on a sudden occasion, they will either perish of his violence or betray him. No man can decree the value of one word, unless it is his own invention; the value which it will have in his hands has been decreed by his own past, by the past of his race. It is, of course, impossible to study words too deeply, though all men are not born for this study: but Pater's influence has tended to encourage meticulosity in detail and single words, rather than a regard for form in its largest sense.

His words and still less his disciples' have not been lived with sufficiently. Unless a man write with his whole nature concentrated upon his subject he is unlikely to take hold of another man.' (*Walter Pater* pp. 215–16)

With this ideal before him, and given the friendly boost of Frost's self-confident encouragement, it seems inevitable that, once Edward Thomas had committed himself solely to verse writing, the mislaid key would be found and the 'great treasure-house', that he later promised to his wife (in Poem 109) would become freely available to others.

## IV

When they are read chronologically the poems seem to fall readily into six groups: (1) Poems 1–16, composed between November 1914 and 1 January 1915; (2) Poems 17–75, written at speed between 1 January and 24 May 1915 when Thomas was finishing his *Life of the Duke of Marlborough* and considering some form of non-military employment; (3) Poems 76–85, written between 25 June and his enlistment in the Artists' Rifles on 14 July 1915; (4) Poems 86–93, the first Service-poems, composed between 21 July and 26 December 1915; (5) Poems 94–128, written either in London or in camp (or on short leaves) at Hare Hall where the poet was a map-reading N.C.O. instructor; (6) Poems 129–144, poems written after he had applied at Hare Hall for a commission in the Royal Artillery, or during his final training as a Gunnery officer, or on various embarkation leaves.

The first group of poems suggest that Thomas closely followed Frost's advice to base his experiments in verse on passages selected from his earlier prose or from previously unpublished prose sketches. Yet already in 'March', 'Old Man', and 'After Rain', the poet concentrates the inner movement of each poem around a single, clearly observed moment of perception. The sudden gush of versifying that followed in the first five months of 1915 produced an uneven mixture of some fine poems and a great deal of apprentice work. Some verses read to me like abandoned first drafts of poems he never returned to: most of them, in their various draft stages, suggest a craftsman confident of his skill but impatient of failure. Enough quality survived among these first 75 poems to establish his sudden emergence as a poet in 1917 (under the pseudonym of 'Edward Eastaway') and a few of them (for example, 'Lob', 'Wind and Mist', 'Beauty', 'Health', 'Parting', 'Home I', 'The Path' and 'The Chalk-Pit') would find their place in any anthology of early twentieth-century English verse.

When these poems were finished, I believe that Thomas had already decided to enlist as a soldier. The ten pre-enlistment poems that follow capture the attitude of many civilians to the first phase of the war in 1915. From the personal 'I built myself a house of glass', through 'Words', the first sonnet for Frost ('A Dream') and the eerie 'Aspens', to 'For these [Prayer]', the poet seems to be casting up the account of his past life as a man and writer:

> For these I ask not, but, neither too late
> Nor yet too early, for what men call content,
> And also that something may be sent
> To be contented with, I ask of fate.

The early poems of an enlisted man that follow are not remarkable except as a gloss on his immediate response to minor incidents in camp or at his parents' home in Balham, where he had begun life as a young writer and was now billeted. In them one can detect a tenuous connection with his pre-military life but, as the poem 'Roads' suggests, his ready acceptance of the pattern of frequent visits home during short leaves from duty is beginning to replace the restless, wandering despair of the two years before 1914 as a focus for an even deeper probe into his earlier self. He appears now to find assurance from the haunting presence of a new kind of future which he has to share with others:

> Now all roads lead to France
> And heavy is the tread
> Of the living; but the dead
> Returning lightly dance.

This renewed impetus to further introspection, and not the mere accident of his being sick and irritable with a chill at his parents' home, triggered off the sequence of honest poems (99–109) which uncover sparely his complicated attitude to the demands of love and affection, especially in his relationship to his parents, his wife and his three children. At the same time he scrutinizes the nature of friendship, especially the new, enforced companionship of life in barracks—a dim echo of his Oxford years—and the many days spent almost exclusively with Robert Frost in Gloucestershire in 1914 (Poem 119). From then onwards—as was his wont with all vital personal decisions—he slowly pondered his growing desire to seek a commission leading almost inevitably, in the summer of 1916, along the road to France. The ecstatic poem, 'After you speak', written on the way home to Steep from Hare Hall Camp, seems to put an end, quite unequivocally, to this mature search for a key to the mysterious truth he experienced in physical love:

> Like a black star
> He seems—
> A mote
> Of singing dust
> Afloat
> Above,
> That dreams
> And sheds no light.
> I know your lust
> Is love.

During the summer of 1916 the news of the Somme filtered through to his training camp much more starkly than in the newspaper accounts that reached his civilian friends and family, and becomes a recognizable and ominous undertone to his remaining poems. Even the apparently mock nursery rhyme, 'The Gallows', can be read as a triple gloss—on a gamekeeper's gallows, on the house of that name where Frost had stayed after late August 1914 at Ryton near Dymock, and on the barbed wire entanglements of the Front Line.

V

Three quotations from an article on 'War Poetry' that Thomas wrote in December 1914 give some indication of the civilian writer's deep response to the onset of the Great War and suggest clairvoyantly how these last poems in 1916 may still be read and interpreted:

I need hardly say that by becoming ripe for poetry the poet's thoughts may recede far from their original resemblance to all the world's, and may seem to have little to do with daily events. They may retain hardly any colour from 1798 [a reference to Thomas's preference for Coleridge's 'Fears in Solitude'] or 1914, and the crowd, deploring it, will naturally not read the poems.

Very seldom are poems written for occasions, great or small, more seldom for great than for small. But verses are, and they may be excellent. Virtually all hymns are occasional verses. They are written for certain people or a certain class. The writer of hymns or verses appears to be a man who feels himself always or at the time one with the class, perhaps the whole nation, or he is a smart fellow who can simulate or exaggerate this sympathy. Experience, reality, truth, unless suffused or submerged by popular sentiment, are out of place.

Mr. Hardy has written an impersonal song which seems to me the best of the time, as it is the least particular and occasional. He may even write better yet. I should also expect the work of other real poets to improve as the war advances, perhaps after it is over, as they understand it and themselves more completely.

Almost exactly twelve months after he wrote the ecstatic 'Words' (in late June 1915), Edward Thomas began to write his last seventeen poems which testify to the progress he had made in understanding himself and the War more completely. Six of these poems ('The Green Roads', 'The Gallows', 'Blenheim Oranges', (i.e. 'Gone, gone again'), 'The Trumpet', 'Lights Out', 'Out in the dark') seem to provide the most tangible evidence we can possibly have—apart from his War Diary—of the manner in which his poetry would have developed. His penultimate poem, 'Out in the dark', with its four stanzas each of five lines linked together by a single rhyme, is a magnificent virtuoso performance that combines a particular occasion with a life-time of experience and moves at times swiftly between poised moments of stillness. On the surface it can be read as a hesitant, almost pessimistic acceptance of his inevitable death in France. But the final stanza is an affirmation of the joy to be found in the simple, primitive things of ordinary experience, a courageous invitation to go forward without fear, sustained by clear truth and not by false hope:

> How weak and little is the light,
> All the universe of sight,

> Love and delight,
> Before the might,
> If you love it not, of night.

The War Diary too shows that the mood and the concept of life which underpin his most mature poetry were adequate to sustain the extreme demands made upon his sensitive nature by the front-line war in France. Experience, thoroughly sifted, and poetry, achieved through a rigorous discarding of verbal excess, came together.

More pragmatic than Yeats, and as critically self-assured as Eliot later became about the potential imprecision inherent in any rigorous use of language, the absence of Edward Thomas's voice in the decade after 1920 was a severe gap in many readers' experience of poetry. In 1936 Yeats included only one of his poems, the least representative, in *The Oxford Book of Modern Verse 1892–1935*; thirty-six years later, Dame Helen Gardner selected six admirable poems for *The New Oxford Book of English Verse (1250–1950)*. The anthologist has an unenviable task to perform. I believe the reader who adds some of Thomas's poems to his own private anthology will find in them convincing proof of the now accepted significance of a voice that speaks, as he would have wished,

> Fixed and free
> In a rhyme,
> As poets do.

# BIOGRAPHICAL OUTLINE[1]

| 1878 | 3 March | Philip Edward Thomas born at Lambeth in London, the eldest of six sons of Philip Henry and Mary Elizabeth Thomas. |
| 1883–93 | | Attends various board-schools, private schools, and Battersea Grammar School. |
| 1894 | January | Enters St. Paul's School. A frequent visitor to home of James Ashcroft Noble. |
| 1895 | Easter | Leaves St. Paul's. Essays published in various journals. Friendship with Helen Noble. |
| 1896 | April–September | Works first for Civil Service Examination and then for entry to Oxford University. |
| 1897 | | His first book, *The Woodland Life*, published. |
| | October | Matriculates as a non-collegiate student at Oxford; lodgings at 113 Cowley Road. |
| 1898 | March | Wins a history scholarship to Lincoln College. Continues his journalism during Oxford career. |
| 1899 | June | Edward and Helen married in London at Fulham Registry Office. |
| 1900 | January | His son, Merfyn, born. Gordon Bottomley begins his correspondence with Helen and Edward. |
| | Summer | Gains a 2nd Class in Final Honours History Schools. Decides to become a writer and not enter the Civil Service. |
| | August– | Penurious existence as a writer, first at Atheldene Road, Earlsfield, and then at 7 Nightingale |
| 1901 | August | Parade, Balham, S. London. |
| | September | Moves to Rose Acre Cottage (one mile outside Bearsted), near Maidstone, Kent. |
| 1902 | October | Elder daughter, Bronwen, born. |
| | November | Becomes a regular reviewer for *Daily Chronicle* on the death of Lionel Johnson. |

[1] For a more detailed account see *Eckert, Cooke, GB, Moore*. For a list of his publications see *GB*, pp. 287–90.

| 1903 | February | First commissioned book, *Oxford*. |
| | July | Moves to cottage on Bearsted Green. |
| | September | Consults a specialist about ill health and exhaustion. |
| 1904 | May | Moves to Elses Farm, The Weald, near Sevenoaks, Kent. Continues reviewing and works on *Beautiful Wales* (second commission). |
| 1905 | Summer | Physically and mentally exhausted. Experiments with 'ejaculations in prose'. |
| | October | Invites W. H. Davies to share his small study cottage. |
| 1906 | | Meets W. H. Hudson, Walter de la Mare. |
| | April–July | Walking tours; more reviewing; more commissioned books. |
| | October | Notice to quit Elses Farm. Stays in London. |
| | November | Regular reviewer for Hilaire Belloc with *Morning Post*. |
| | December | Moves to Berryfield Cottage, Ashford, Petersfield, near to Bedales School. |
| 1907 | April | Visits a specialist about his 'melancholia'. |
| | August | Walking tour with Helen in 'Jefferies Country'. |
| 1908 | January–February | First draft of *Richard Jefferies* completed at Minsmere, near Dunwich, Suffolk. |
| | August–December | Assistant Secretary to a Royal Commission on Welsh Monuments. Lives in London; continues to review and write books; resigns for health reasons. |
| 1909 | January | Returns to Ashford where a new house is planned. |
| | April | Enters new study at top of Ashford Hanger; work begins on new house. |
| | Autumn | Merfyn and Bronwen attend Bedales; Helen teaches there in the Kindergarten. |
| | Before Christmas | Moves into new house, Wick Green, Petersfield, Hampshire. |
| 1910 | | Continues to write books and to review for *Daily Chronicle*, *Morning Post*, *Saturday Review*, and *The Bookman*. |
| | August | Second daughter, Myfanwy, born. |
| | September | Cycling tour with Merfyn. Visits Conrad, Belloc, Ralph Hodgson, Rupert Brooke. |

| 1911 | January | Follows a strict vegetarian diet. |
| | March | Low in health and spirit. |
| | April–August | At work on six books of various kinds. |
| | September | Severe breakdown caused by overwork and financial worry. |
| | October–December | In West Wales and Laugharne; writes *George Borrow*. |
| 1912 | January | Begins fortnightly visits to London in search of literary work. Writes for H. Monro's *Poetry Review*. |
| | April | Stays with Clifford Bax in Somerset and is treated by Godwin Baynes (a nerve specialist). |
| | May–June | Near Bath. Treatment and writing continue. |
| | July | Begins reviewing for *The English Review* and *The Nation*. |
| | August | Cycles with Merfyn in Somerset and Kent. |
| | November | Leaves Wick Green; stays with Vivian Locke Ellis as a paying guest at Selsfield House, East Grinstead. Writes *Walter Pater*. Begins fiction, *The Happy-Go-Lucky Morgans*. Meets Eleanor Farjeon. |
| 1913 | January–February | His health much worse. Travels a great deal in Wiltshire and Somerset, preparing *In Pursuit of Spring*. |
| | March–May | At work on various books, reviewing for monthlies, quarterlies, and *Daily Chronicle*. |
| | July | Sells books before moving to a small cottage (Yew-tree Cottage) in Steep village, near Petersfield. |
| | August | Moves to Steep village; retains hill-top study. |
| | October | Introduced to Robert Frost by Ralph Hodgson. |
| | December | Begins his autobiography at Selsfield House, East Grinstead, Sussex. Meets Frost again. |
| 1914 | January–February | Chiefly in London; working on his autobiography. |
| | March | In Steep, reviewing, proof-reading, writing articles. |
| | April | Travels to Wales and then to see Frost in Herefordshire. *In Pursuit of Spring* published. |
| | June | At Cartmel with Bottomley, then Herefordshire with Frost. |

| | July | Reviews Frost's *North of Boston*. Helen and Edward visit Frost at Ledington. |
|---|---|---|
| | August | Thomases on holiday with Frosts at Ledington. |
| | September | Cycling tour in Midlands and the north of England, preparing articles for *The English Review*. Visits Frost and plans to leave with him for U.S.A. |
| | October | Monthly and quarterly reviewing. Cycling in Wales and then back to Ledington. |
| | November–December | At Steep, begins prose versions of earliest poems. Earliest poems written and sent to Frost. |
| 1915 | January | Confined to Steep with severely sprained ankle. Writing poetry. Eleanor Farjeon begins to type them. |
| | February | Unable to walk. Merfyn leaves with Frosts for U.S.A. Thomas sends poems to friends and, unsuccessfully, to some editors. Adopts pseudonym of 'Edward Eastaway' for his verse. |
| | March–June | Writing poetry and *The Life of the Duke of Marlborough*. Preparing anthology *This England* for the press. |
| | July | Enlists in the Artists' Rifles. Poems sent to Bottomley for inclusion in *An Annual of New Poetry*. |
| | August–September | Billeted with his parents at Balham. |
| | October | In camp at High Beech, near Loughton, Essex. |
| | November | Moved to Hare Hall Camp, Gidea Park, Romford. Promoted to Lance-Corporal. Acting as map-reading instructor. |
| | December | Merfyn returns from U.S.A. |
| 1916 | January | Still at Hare Hall Camp. |
| | February | A convalescent leave spent at Steep. |
| | March | Promoted to Corporal. Frequent leaves; continues to write verse. *Keats* published. |
| | June | Awarded a £300 grant instead of a Civil List Pension. Applies for a commission in the Royal Artillery. Asked to leave his study at Steep. |
| | July | Granted £1 a week by the Civil Liability Commission (to cease if he becomes an officer). Declines to stay on the permanent staff at Hare Hall Camp. |

| | | |
|---|---|---|
| | August | Roger Ingpen considers publication of a selection of his verse. |
| | September | An officer cadet with the R.A. in London. Stays often with his parents at Balham, begins to arrange the typescripts of his poems. Moves his family to High Beech, near Loughton, Essex. |
| | October | Moved to firing camp in Wiltshire, near Trowbridge. |
| | November | Commissioned 2nd Lieutenant; posted to 244 Siege Battery, R.G.A. Lydd, Kent. Visits Cartmel and Gloucester before returning to High Beech. |
| | December | Volunteers for service overseas. Sees proofs of *An Annual of New Poetry*. Sends duplicate set of poems [*EE*] to Frost. |
| 1917[2] | January | Embarkation leave, then final firing practice at Codford, near Warminster, Wiltshire. |
| | 13 January | 'Last poem' written in his diary. |
| | 29 January | Embarkation from Southampton. |
| | 4 February | Leaves Le Havre area for front line. |
| | 11 February | Settles into positions near Arras. |
| | 9 March | After a spell at Group H.Q. returns to his Battery. Begins duty at the Observation Post (Ronville). |
| | 26 March– | Positions moved up beyond Achicourt in preparation for forthcoming 'Battle of Arras'. |
| | 8 April | Under constant artillery fire. |
| | 9 April | On duty at the Observation Post. Killed by the blast of a shell at 7.36 a.m. during the first hour of the Arras 'offensive'. |

[2]For a detailed account of Thomas's last ninety-eight days as a soldier see Appendix, pp.173 – 94.

# POEMS

## 1914–1917

# 1914

---

## *Up in the Wind*

'I could wring the old thing's neck that put it there!
A public-house! it may be public for birds,
Squirrels and suchlike, ghosts of charcoal-burners
And highwaymen.' The wild girl laughed. 'But I
Hate it since I came back from Kennington.                    5
I gave up a good place.' Her cockney accent
Made her and the house seem wilder by calling up—
Only to be subdued at once by wildness—
The idea of London there in that forest parlour,
Low and small among those towering beeches                   10
And the one bulging butt that's like a font.

Her eyes flashed up; she shook her hair away
From eyes and mouth, as if to shriek again;
Then sighed back to her scrubbing. While I drank
I might have mused of coaches and highwaymen,                15
Charcoal-burners and life that loves the wild.
For who now used these roads except myself,
A market waggon every other Wednesday,
A solitary tramp, some very fresh one
Ignorant of these eleven houseless miles,                    20
A motorist from a distance slowing down
To taste whatever luxury he can
In having North Downs clear behind, South clear before,
And being midway between two railway lines
Far out of sight or sound of them? There are                 25
Some houses—down the by-lanes; and a few
Are visible—when their damsons are in bloom.
But the land is wild, and there's a spirit of wildness
Much older, crying when the stone-curlew yodels
His sea and mountain cry, high up in Spring.                 30

He nests in fields where still the gorse is free as
When all was open and common. Common 'tis named
And calls itself, because the bracken and gorse
Still hold the hedge where plough and scythe have chased them.
Once on a time 'tis plain that the 'White Horse'                    35
Stood merely on the border of a waste
Where horse or cart picked its own course afresh.
On all sides then, as now, paths ran to the inn;
And now a farm-track takes you from a gate.

Two roads cross, and not a house in sight                          40
Except the 'White Horse' in this clump of beeches.
It hides from either road, a field's breadth back;
And it's the trees you see, and not the house,
Both near and far, when the clump's the highest thing
And homely too upon a far horizon                                  45
To one who knows there is an inn within.

' 'Twould have been different' the wild girl shrieked, 'suppose
That widow had married another blacksmith and
Kept on the business. This parlour was the smithy.
If she had done, there might never have been an inn:               50
And I, in that case, might never have been born.
Years ago, when this was all a wood
And the smith had charcoal-burners for company,
A man from a beech-country in the shires
Came with an engine and a little boy                               55
(To feed the engine) to cut up timber here.
It all happened years ago. The smith
Had died, his widow had set up an alehouse—
I could wring the old thing's neck for thinking of it.
Well, I suppose they fell in love, the widow                       60
And my great-uncle that sawed up the timber:
Leastways they married. The little boy stayed on.
He was my father.' She thought she'd scrub again,
—'I draw the ale, and he grows fat' she muttered—
But only studied the hollows in the bricks                         65
And chose among her thoughts in stirring silence.
The clock ticked, and the big saucepan lid

Heaved as the cabbage bubbled, and the girl
Questioned the fire and spoke: 'My father, he
Took to the land. A mile of it is worth                                    70
A guinea; for by that time all the trees
Except those few about the house were gone.
That's all that's left of the forest unless you count
The bottoms of the charcoal-burners' fires—
We plough one up at times. Did you ever see                                75
Our signboard?' No. The post and empty frame
I knew. Without them I could not have guessed
The low grey house and its one stack under trees
Was not a hermitage but a public-house.
'But can that empty frame be any use?                                      80
Now I should like to see a good white horse
Swing there, a really beautiful white horse,
Galloping one side, being painted on the other.'
'But would you like to hear it swing all night
And all day? All I ever had to thank                                       85
The wind for was for blowing the sign down.
Time after time it blew down and I could sleep.
At last they fixed it, and it took a thief
To move it, and we've never had another:
It's lying at the bottom of our pond.                                      90
But no one's moved the wood from off the hill
There at the back, although it makes a noise
When the wind blows, as if a train was running
The other side, a train that never stops
Or ends. And the linen crackles on the line                               95
Like a woodfire rising.' 'But if you had the sign
You might draw company. What about Kennington?'
She bent down to her scrubbing with 'Not me.
Not back to Kennington. Here I was born,
And I've a notion on these windy nights                                    100
Here I shall die. Perhaps I want to die here.
I reckon I shall stay. But I do wish
The road was nearer and the wind farther off,
Or once now and then quite still, though when I die
I'd have it blowing that I might go with it                                105
Somewhere far off, where there are trees no more

And I could wake and not know where I was
Nor even wonder if they would roar again.
Look at those calves.'

               Between the open door
And the trees two calves were wading in the pond,     110
Grazing the water here and there and thinking,
Sipping and thinking, both happily, neither long.
The water wrinkled, but they sipped and thought,
As careless of the wind as it of us.
'Look at those calves. Hark at the trees again.'     115


## 2

## *November Sky*

November's days are thirty:
November's earth is dirty,
Those thirty days, from first to last;
And the prettiest things on ground are the paths
With morning and evening hobnails dinted,     5
With foot and wing-tip overprinted
Or separately charactered,
Of little beast and little bird.
The fields are mashed by sheep, the roads
Make the worst going, the best the woods     10
Where dead leaves upward and downward scatter.
Few care for the mixture of earth and water,
Twig, leaf, flint, thorn,
Straw, feather, all that men scorn,
Pounded up and sodden by flood,     15
Condemned as mud.

But of all the months when earth is greener
Not one has clean skies that are cleaner.
Clean and clear and sweet and cold,
They shine above the earth so old,     20

While the after-tempest cloud
Sails over in silence though winds are loud,
Till the full moon in the east
Looks at the planet in the west
And earth is silent as it is black,                          25
Yet not unhappy for its lack.
Up from the dirty earth men stare:
One imagines a refuge there
Above the mud, in the pure bright
Of the cloudless heavenly light:                            30
Another loves earth and November more dearly
Because without them, he sees clearly,
The sky would be nothing more to his eye
Than he, in any case, is to the sky;
He loves even the mud whose dyes                            35
Renounce all brightness to the skies.

## 3

## *March*

Now I know that Spring will come again,
Perhaps tomorrow: however late I've patience
After this night following on such a day.

While still my temples ached from the cold burning
Of hail and wind, and still the primroses                    5
Torn by the hail were covered up in it,
The sun filled earth and heaven with a great light
And a tenderness, almost warmth, where the hail dripped,
As if the mighty sun wept tears of joy.
But 'twas too late for warmth. The sunset piled            10
Mountains on mountains of snow and ice in the west:
Somewhere among their folds the wind was lost,
And yet 'twas cold, and though I knew that Spring
Would come again, I knew it had not come,
That it was lost, too, in those mountains cold.            15

What did the thrushes know? Rain, snow, sleet, hail,
Had kept them quiet as the primroses.
They had but an hour to sing. On boughs they sang,
On gates, on ground; they sang while they changed perches
And while they fought, if they remembered to fight:     20
So earnest were they to pack into that hour
Their unwilling hoard of song before the moon
Grew brighter than the clouds. Then 'twas no time
For singing merely. So they could keep off silence
And night, they cared not what they sang or screamed,   25
Whether 'twas hoarse or sweet or fierce or soft,
And to me all was sweet: they could do no wrong.
Something they knew—I also, while they sang
And after. Not till night had half its stars
And never a cloud, was I aware of silence     30
Rich with all that riot of songs, a silence
Saying that Spring returns, perhaps tomorrow.

# 4

## *Old Man*

Old Man, or Lad's-love,—in the name there's nothing
To one that knows not Lad's-love, or Old Man,
The hoar-green feathery herb, almost a tree,
Growing with rosemary and lavender.
Even to one that knows it well, the names     5
Half decorate, half perplex, the thing it is:
At least, what that is clings not to the names
In spite of time. And yet I like the names.

The herb itself I like not, but for certain
I love it, as some day the child will love it     10
Who plucks a feather from the door-side bush
Whenever she goes in or out of the house.
Often she waits there, snipping the tips and shrivelling
The shreds at last on to the path, perhaps

Thinking, perhaps of nothing, till she sniffs      15
Her fingers and runs off. The bush is still
But half as tall as she, though it is as old;
So well she clips it. Not a word she says;
And I can only wonder how much hereafter
She will remember, with that bitter scent,      20
Of garden rows, and ancient damson-trees
Topping a hedge, a bent path to a door,
A low thick bush beside the door, and me
Forbidding her to pick.

               As for myself,
Where first I met the bitter scent is lost.      25
I, too, often shrivel the grey shreds,
Sniff them and think and sniff again and try
Once more to think what it is I am remembering,
Always in vain. I cannot like the scent,
Yet I would rather give up others more sweet,      30
With no meaning, than this bitter one.

I have mislaid the key. I sniff the spray
And think of nothing; I see and I hear nothing;
Yet seem, too, to be listening, lying in wait
For what I should, yet never can, remember:      35
No garden appears, no path, no hoar-green bush
Of Lad's-love, or Old Man, no child beside,
Neither father nor mother, nor any playmate;
Only an avenue, dark, nameless, without end.

5

*The Signpost*

The dim sea glints chill. The white sun is shy,
And the skeleton weeds and the never-dry,
Rough, long grasses keep white with frost
At the hilltop by the finger-post;

The smoke of traveller's-joy is puffed          5
Over hawthorn berry and hazel tuft.

I read the sign. Which way shall I go?
A voice says: You would not have doubted so
At twenty. Another voice gentle with scorn
Says: At twenty you wished you had never been born.    10

One hazel lost a leaf of gold
From a tuft at the tip, when the first voice told
The other he wished to know what 'twould be
To be sixty by this same post. 'You shall see'
He laughed—and I had to join his laughter—    15
'You shall see; but either before or after,
Whatever happens, it must befall,
A mouthful of earth to remedy all
Regrets and wishes shall freely be given;
And if there be a flaw in that heaven    20
'Twill be freedom to wish, and your wish may be
To be here or anywhere talking to me,
No matter what the weather, on earth,
At any age between death and birth,
To see what day or night can be,    25
The sun and the frost, the land and the sea,
Summer, Autumn, Winter, Spring,
With a poor man of any sort, down to a king,
Standing upright out in the air
Wondering where he shall journey, O where?'    30

# 6

## *The Other*

The forest ended. Glad I was
To feel the light, and hear the hum
Of bees, and smell the drying grass
And the sweet mint, because I had come

To an end of forest, and because          5
Here was both road and inn, the sum
Of what's not forest. But 'twas here
They asked me if I did not pass
Yesterday this way? 'Not you? Queer.'
'Who then? and slept here?' I felt fear.          10

I learnt his road and, ere they were
Sure I was I, left the dark wood
Behind, kestrel and woodpecker,
The inn in the sun, the happy mood
When first I tasted sunlight there.          15
I travelled fast, in hopes I should
Outrun that other. What to do
When caught, I planned not. I pursued
To prove the likeness, and, if true,
To watch until myself I knew.          20

I tried the inns that evening
Of a long gabled high-street grey,
Of courts and outskirts, travelling
An eager but a weary way,
In vain. He was not there. Nothing          25
Told me that ever till that day
Had one like me entered those doors,
Save once. That time I dared: 'You may
Recall'—but never-foamless shores
Make better friends than those dull boors.          30

Many and many a day like this
Aimed at the unseen moving goal
And nothing found but remedies
For all desire. These made not whole;
They sowed a new desire, to kiss          35
Desire's self beyond control,
Desire of desire. And yet
Life stayed on within my soul.
One night in sheltering from the wet
I quite forgot I could forget.          40

A customer, then the landlady
Stared at me. With a kind of smile
They hesitated awkwardly:
Their silence gave me time for guile.
Had anyone called there like me,                    45
I asked. It was quite plain the wile
Succeeded. For they poured out all.
And that was naught. Less than a mile
Beyond the inn, I could recall
He was like me in general.                          50

He had pleased them, but I less.
I was more eager than before
To find him out and to confess,
To bore him and to let him bore.
I could not wait: children might guess              55
I had a purpose, something more
That made an answer indiscreet.
One girl's caution made me sore,
Too indignant even to greet
That other had we chanced to meet.                  60

I sought then in solitude.
The wind had fallen with the night; as still
The roads lay as the ploughland rude,
Dark and naked, on the hill.
Had there been ever any feud                        65
'Twixt earth and sky, a mighty will
Closed it: the crocketed dark trees,
A dark house, dark impossible
Cloud-towers, one star, one lamp, one peace
Held on an everlasting lease:                       70

And all was earth's, or all was sky's;
No difference endured between
The two. A dog barked on a hidden rise;
A marshbird whistled high unseen;
The latest waking blackbird's cries                 75
Perished upon the silence keen.

12

The last light filled a narrow firth
Among the clouds. I stood serene,
And with a solemn quiet mirth,
An old inhabitant of earth.                           80

Once the name I gave to hours
Like this was melancholy, when
It was not happiness and powers
Coming like exiles home again,
And weakness quitting their bowers,                   85
Smiled and enjoyed, far off from men,
Moments of everlastingness.
And fortunate my search was then
While what I sought, nevertheless,
That I was seeking, I did not guess.                  90

That time was brief: once more at inn
And upon road I sought my man
Till once amid a tap-room's din
Loudly he asked for me, began
To speak, as if it had been a sin,                    95
Of how I thought and dreamed and ran
After him thus, day after day:
He lived as one under a ban
For this: what had I got to say?
I said nothing. I slipped away.                       100

And now I dare not follow after
Too close. I try to keep in sight,
Dreading his frown and worse his laughter.
I steal out of the wood to light;
I see the swift shoot from the rafter                 105
By the inn door: ere I alight
I wait and hear the starlings wheeze
And nibble like ducks: I wait his flight.
He goes: I follow: no release
Until he ceases. Then I also shall cease.             110

# 7

## *After Rain*

The rain of a night and a day and a night
Stops at the light
Of this pale choked day. The peering sun
Sees what has been done.
The road under the trees has a border new     5
Of purple hue
Inside the border of bright thin grass:
For all that has
Been left by November of leaves is torn
From hazel and thorn     10
And the greater trees. Throughout the copse
No dead leaf drops
On grey grass, green moss, burnt-orange fern,
At the wind's return:
The leaflets out of the ash-tree shed     15
Are thinly spread
In the road, like little black fish, inlaid,
As if they played.
What hangs from the myriad branches down there
So hard and bare     20
Is twelve yellow apples lovely to see
On one crab-tree,
And on each twig of every tree in the dell
Uncountable
Crystals both dark and bright of the rain     25
That begins again.

# 8

## *Interval*

Gone the wild day.
A wilder night

Coming makes way
For brief twilight.

Where the firm soaked road                  5
Mounts beneath pines
To the high beech wood
It almost shines.

The beeches keep
A stormy rest,                               10
Breathing deep
Of wind from the west.

The wood is black,
With a misty steam.
Above it the rack                            15
Breaks for one gleam.

But the woodman's cot
By the ivied trees
Awakens not
To light or breeze.                          20

It smokes aloft
Unwavering:
It hunches soft
Under storm's wing.

It has no care                               25
For gleam or gloom:
It stays there
While I shall roam,

Die and forget
The hill of trees,                           30
The gleam, the wet,
This roaring peace.

## 9

### *Birds' Nests*

The summer nests uncovered by autumn wind,
Some torn, others dislodged, all dark,
Everyone sees them: low or high in tree,
Or hedge, or single bush, they hang like a mark.

Since there's no need of eyes to see them with            5
I cannot help a little shame
That I missed most, even at eye's level, till
The leaves blew off and made the seeing no game.

'Tis a light pang. I like to see the nests
Still in their places, now first known,                  10
At home and by far roads. Boys never found them,
Whatever jays or squirrels may have done.

And most I like the winter nest deep-hid
That leaves and berries fell into;
Once a dormouse dined there on hazel nuts;               15
And grass and goose-grass seeds found soil and grew.

## 10

### *The Mountain Chapel*

Chapel and gravestones, old and few,
Are shrouded by a mountain fold
From sound and view
Of life. The loss of the brook's voice
Falls like a shadow. All they hear is                    5
The eternal noise
Of wind whistling in grass more shrill
Than aught as human as a sword,
And saying still:

'  'Tis but a moment since man's birth,                    10
And in another moment more
Man lies in earth
For ever; but I am the same
Now, and shall be, even as I was
Before he came:                                           15
Till there is nothing I shall be.'

Yet there the sun shines after noon
So cheerfully
The place almost seems peopled, nor
Lacks cottage chimney, cottage hearth:                    20
It is not more
In size than is a cottage, less
Than any other empty home
In homeliness.
It has a garden of wild flowers                           25
And finest grass and gravestones warm
In sunshine hours
The year through. Men behind the glass
Stand once a week, singing, and drown
The whistling grass                                       30
Their ponies munch. And yet somewhere
Near or far off there's some man could
Live happy here,
Or one of the gods perhaps, were they
Not of inhuman stature dire                               35
As poets say
Who have not seen them clearly, if
At sound of any wind of the world
In grass-blades stiff
They would not startle and shudder cold                   40
Under the sun. When Gods were young
This wind was old.

## I I

## *The Manor Farm*

The rock-like mud unfroze a little and rills
Ran and sparkled down each side of the road
Under the catkins wagging in the hedge.
But earth would have her sleep out, spite of the sun;
Nor did I value that thin gilding beam      5
More than a pretty February thing
Till I came down to the old Manor Farm,
And church and yew-tree opposite, in age
Its equals and in size. Small church, great yew,
And farmhouse slept in a Sunday silentness.      10
The air raised not a straw. The steep farm roof,
With tiles duskily glowing, entertained
The midday sun; and up and down the roof
White pigeons nestled. There was no sound but one.
Three cart-horses were looking over a gate      15
Drowsily through their forelocks, swishing their tails
Against a fly, a solitary fly.

The Winter's cheek flushed as if he had drained
Spring, Summer, and Autumn at a draught
And smiled quietly. But 'twas not Winter—      20
Rather a season of bliss unchangeable
Awakened from farm and church where it had lain
Safe under tile and thatch for ages since
This England, Old already, was called Merry.

## I 2

## *An Old Song* [1]

I was not apprenticed nor ever dwelt in famous Lincolnshire;
I've served one master ill and well much more than seven year;

And never took up to poaching as you shall quickly find;
    But 'tis my delight of a shiny night in the season of the year.

I roamed where nobody had a right but keepers and squires,    5
    and there
I sought for nests, wild flowers, oak sticks, and moles, both
    far and near,
And had to run from farmers, and learnt the Lincolnshire song:
    'Oh, 'tis my delight of a shiny night in the season of the year.'

I took those walks years after, talking with friend or dear,
Or solitary musing; but when the moon shone clear    10
I had no joy or sorrow that could not be expressed
    By ''Tis my delight of a shiny night in the season of the year.'

Since then I've thrown away a chance to fight a gamekeeper;
And I less often trespass, and what I see or hear
Is mostly from the road or path by day: yet still I sing:    15
    'Oh, 'tis my delight of a shiny night in the season of the year.'

For if I am contented, at home or anywhere,
Or if I sigh for I know not what, or my heart beats with some fear,
It is a strange kind of delight to sing or whistle just:
    'Oh, 'tis my delight of a shiny night in the season of the year.'    20

And with this melody on my lips and no one by to care,
Indoors, or out on shiny nights or dark in open air,
I am for a moment made a man that sings out of his heart:
    'Oh, 'tis my delight of a shiny night in the season of the year.'

# 13

## *An Old Song* [2]

The sun set, the wind fell, the sea
Was like a mirror shaking:
The one small wave that clapped the land

A mile-long snake of foam was making
Where tide had smoothed and wind had dried                         5
The vacant sand.

A light divided the swollen clouds
And lay most perfectly
Like a straight narrow footbridge bright
That crossed over the sea to me;                                  10
And no one else in the whole world
Saw that same sight.

I walked elate, my bridge always
Just one step from my feet:
A robin sang, a shade in shade:                                   15
And all I did was to repeat:
    'I'll go no more a-roving
    With you, fair maid.'

The sailors' song of merry loving
With dusk and sea-gull's mewing                                   20
Mixed sweet, the lewdness far outweighed
By the wild charm the chorus played:
    'I'll go no more a-roving
    With you, fair maid:
    A-roving, a-roving, since roving's been my ruin,             25
    I'll go no more a-roving with you, fair maid.'

*In Amsterdam there dwelt a maid—*
*Mark well what I do say—*
*In Amsterdam there dwelt a maid*
*And she was a mistress of her trade:*                            30
*I'll go no more a-roving*
*With you, fair maid:*
*A-roving, a-roving, since roving's been my ruin,*
*I'll go no more a-roving with you, fair maid.*

## 14

### *The Combe*

The Combe was ever dark, ancient and dark.
Its mouth is stopped with bramble, thorn, and briar;
And no one scrambles over the sliding chalk
By beech and yew and perishing juniper
Down the half precipices of its sides, with roots          5
And rabbit holes for steps. The sun of Winter,
The moon of Summer, and all the singing birds
Except the missel-thrush that loves juniper,
Are quite shut out. But far more ancient and dark
The Combe looks since they killed the badger there,        10
Dug him out and gave him to the hounds,
That most ancient Briton of English beasts.


## 15

### *The Hollow Wood*

Out in the sun the goldfinch flits
Along the thistle-tops, flits and twits
Above the hollow wood
Where birds swim like fish—
Fish that laugh and shriek—                5
To and fro, far below
In the pale hollow wood.

Lichen, ivy, and moss
Keep evergreen the trees
That stand half-flayed and dying,          10
And the dead trees on their knees
In dog's-mercury, ivy, and moss:
And the bright twit of the goldfinch drops
Down there as he flits on thistle-tops.

## 16

### The New Year

He was the one man I met up in the woods
That stormy New Year's morning; and at first sight,
Fifty yards off, I could not tell how much
Of the strange tripod was a man. His body,
Bowed horizontal, was supported equally                          5
By legs at one end, by a rake at the other:
Thus he rested, far less like a man than
His wheel-barrow in profile was like a pig.
But when I saw it was an old man bent,
At the same moment came into my mind                             10
The games at which boys bend thus, *High-cockolorum*,
Or *Fly-the-garter*, and *Leap-frog*. At the sound
Of footsteps he began to straighten himself;
His head rolled under his cape like a tortoise's;
He took an unlit pipe out of his mouth                           15
Politely ere I wished him 'A Happy New Year',
And with his head cast upward sideways muttered—
So far as I could hear through the trees' roar—
'Happy New Year, and may it come fastish, too',
While I strode by and he turned to raking leaves.                20

## 17

### The Source

All day the air triumphs with its two voices
Of wind and rain:
As loud as if in anger it rejoices,
Drowning the sound of earth

That gulps and gulps in choked endeavour vain     5
To swallow the rain.

Half the night, too, only the wild air speaks
With wind and rain,
Till forth the dumb source of the river breaks
And drowns the rain and wind,     10
Bellows like a giant bathing in mighty mirth
The triumph of earth.

## 18

### *The Penny Whistle*

The new moon hangs like an ivory bugle
In the naked frosty blue;
And the ghylls of the forest, already blackened
By Winter, are blackened anew.

The brooks that cut up and increase the forest,     5
As if they had never known
The sun, are roaring with black hollow voices
Betwixt rage and a moan.

But still the caravan-hut by the hollies
Like a kingfisher gleams between:     10
Round the mossed old hearths of the charcoal-burners
First primroses ask to be seen.

The charcoal-burners are black, but their linen
Blows white on the line;
And white the letter the girl is reading     15
Under that crescent fine;

And her brother who hides apart in a thicket,
Slowly and surely playing
On a whistle an olden nursery melody,
Says far more than I am saying.     20

## 19

## *A Private*

This ploughman dead in battle slept out of doors
Many a frosty night, and merrily
Answered staid drinkers, good bedmen, and all bores:
'At Mrs Greenland's Hawthorn Bush,' said he,
'I slept.' None knew which bush. Above the town,    5
Beyond 'The Drover', a hundred spot the down
In Wiltshire. And where now at last he sleeps
More sound in France—that, too, he secret keeps.

## 20

## *Snow*

In the gloom of whiteness,
In the great silence of snow,
A child was sighing
And bitterly saying: 'Oh,
They have killed a white bird up there on her nest,    5
The down is fluttering from her breast.'
And still it fell through that dusky brightness
On the child crying for the bird of the snow.

## 21

## *Adlestrop*

Yes, I remember Adlestrop—
The name, because one afternoon
Of heat the express-train drew up there
Unwontedly. It was late June.

The steam hissed. Someone cleared his throat.   5
No one left and no one came
On the bare platform. What I saw
Was Adlestrop—only the name

And willows, willow-herb, and grass,
And meadowsweet, and haycocks dry,   10
No whit less still and lonely fair
Than the high cloudlets in the sky.

And for that minute a blackbird sang
Close by, and round him, mistier,
Farther and farther, all the birds   15
Of Oxfordshire and Gloucestershire.


## 22

## *Tears*

It seems I have no tears left. They should have fallen—
Their ghosts, if tears have ghosts, did fall—that day
When twenty hounds streamed by me, not yet combed out
But still all equals in their rage of gladness
Upon the scent, made one, like a great dragon   5
In Blooming Meadow that bends towards the sun
And once bore hops: and on that other day
When I stepped out from the double-shadowed Tower
Into an April morning, stirring and sweet
And warm. Strange solitude was there and silence.   10
A mightier charm than any in the Tower
Possessed the courtyard. They were changing guard,
Soldiers in line, young English countrymen,
Fair-haired and ruddy, in white tunics. Drums
And fifes were playing 'The British Grenadiers'.   15
The men, the music piercing that solitude
And silence, told me truths I had not dreamed,
And have forgotten since their beauty passed.

23

## [*Over the Hills*]

Often and often it came back again
To mind, the day I passed the horizon ridge
To a new country, the path I had to find
By half-gaps that were stiles once in the hedge,
The pack of scarlet clouds running across          5
The harvest evening that seemed endless then
And after, and the inn where all were kind,
All were strangers. I did not know my loss
Till one day twelve months later suddenly
I leaned upon my spade and saw it all,            10
Though far beyond the sky-line. It became
Almost a habit through the year for me
To lean and see it and think to do the same
Again for two days and a night. Recall
Was vain: no more could the restless brook        15
Ever turn back and climb the waterfall
To the lake that rests and stirs not in its nook,
As in the hollow of the collar-bone
Under the mountain's head of rush and stone.

24

## *The Lofty Sky*

Today I want the sky,
The tops of the high hills,
Above the last man's house,
His hedges, and his cows,
Where, if I will, I look                            5
Down even on sheep and rook,
And of all things that move
See buzzards only above:—

Past all trees, past furze
And thorn, where naught deters          10
The desire of the eye
For sky, nothing but sky.
I sicken of the woods
And all the multitudes
Of hedge-trees. They are no more          15
Than weeds upon this floor
Of the river of air
Leagues deep, leagues wide, where
I am like a fish that lives
In weeds and mud and gives          20
What's above him no thought.
I might be a tench for aught
That I can do today
Down on the wealden clay.
Even the tench has days          25
When he floats up and plays
Among the lily leaves
And sees the sky, or grieves
Not if he nothing sees:
While I, I know that trees          30
Under that lofty sky
Are weeds, fields mud, and I
Would arise and go far
To where the lilies are.

# 25

## *The Cuckoo*

That's the cuckoo, you say. I cannot hear it.
When last I heard it I cannot recall; but I know
Too well the year when first I failed to hear it—
It was drowned by my man groaning out to his sheep 'Ho! Ho!'

Ten times with an angry voice he shouted          5
'Ho! Ho!' but not in anger, for that was his way.
He died that Summer, and that is how I remember
The cuckoo calling, the children listening, and me saying, 'Nay.'

And now, as you said, 'There it is' I was hearing
Not the cuckoo at all, but my man's 'Ho! Ho!' instead.          10
And I think that even if I could lose my deafness
The cuckoo's note would be drowned by the voice of my dead.


## 26

### *Swedes*

They have taken the gable from the roof of clay
On the long swede pile. They have let in the sun
To the white and gold and purple of curled fronds
Unsunned. It is a sight more tender-gorgeous
At the wood-corner where Winter moans and drips          5
Than when, in the Valley of the Tombs of Kings,
A boy crawls down into a Pharaoh's tomb
And, first of Christian men, beholds the mummy,
God and monkey, chariot and throne and vase,
Blue pottery, alabaster, and gold.          10

But dreamless long-dead Amen-hotep lies.
This is a dream of Winter, sweet as Spring.


## 27

### *The Unknown Bird*

Three lovely notes he whistled, too soft to be heard
If others sang; but others never sang
In the great beech-wood all that May and June.
No one saw him: I alone could hear him
Though many listened. Was it but four years          5
Ago? or five? He never came again.

28

Oftenest when I heard him I was alone,
Nor could I ever make another hear.
La-la-la! he called, seeming far-off—
As if a cock crowed past the edge of the world,                    10
As if the bird or I were in a dream.
Yet that he travelled through the trees and sometimes
Neared me, was plain, though somehow distant still
He sounded. All the proof is—I told men
What I had heard.

     I never knew a voice,                    15
Man, beast, or bird, better than this. I told
The naturalists; but neither had they heard
Anything like the notes that did so haunt me
I had them clear by heart and have them still.
Four years, or five, have made no difference. Then                  20
As now that La-la-la! was bodiless sweet:
Sad more than joyful it was, if I must say
That it was one or other, but if sad
'Twas sad only with joy too, too far off
For me to taste it. But I cannot tell                               25
If truly never anything but fair
The days were when he sang, as now they seem.
This surely I know, that I who listened then,
Happy sometimes, sometimes suffering
A heavy body and a heavy heart,                                     30
Now straightway, if I think of it, become
Light as that bird wandering beyond my shore.


# 28

## *The Mill-Pond*


The sun blazed while the thunder yet
Added a boom:
A wagtail flickered bright over
The mill-pond's gloom:

Less than the cooing in the alder                           5
Isles of the pool
Sounded the thunder through that plunge
Of waters cool.

Scared starlings on the aspen tip
Past the black mill                                        10
Outchattered the stream and the next roar
Far on the hill.

As my feet dangling teased the foam
That slid below
A girl came out. 'Take care!' she said—                   15
Ages ago.

She startled me, standing quite close
Dressed all in white:
Ages ago I was angry till
She passed from sight.                                     20

Then the storm burst, and as I crouched
To shelter, how
Beautiful and kind, too, she seemed,
As she does now!

## 29

### [*Man and Dog*]

' 'Twill take some getting.' 'Sir, I think 'twill so.'
The old man stared up at the mistletoe
That hung too high in the poplar's crest for plunder
Of any climber, though not for kissing under:
Then he went on against the north-east wind—              5
Straight but lame, leaning on a staff new-skinned,
Carrying a brolly, flag-basket, and old coat,—
Towards Alton, ten miles off. And he had not
Done less from Chilgrove where he pulled up docks.

'Twere best, if he had had 'a money-box',                                    10
To have waited there till the sheep cleared a field
For what a half-week's flint-picking would yield.
His mind was running on the work he had done
Since he left Christchurch in the New Forest, one
Spring in the 'seventies,—navvying on dock and line      15
From Southampton to Newcastle-on-Tyne,—
In 'seventy-four a year of soldiering
With the Berkshires,—hoeing and harvesting
In half the shires where corn and couch will grow.
His sons, three sons, were fighting, but the hoe          20
And reap-hook he liked, or anything to do with trees.
He fell once from a poplar tall as these:
The Flying Man they called him in hospital.
'If I flew now, to another world I'd fall.'
He laughed and whistled to the small brown bitch          25
With spots of blue that hunted in the ditch.
Her foxy Welsh grandfather must have paired
Beneath him. He kept sheep in Wales and scared
Strangers, I will warrant, with his pearl eye
And trick of shrinking off as he were shy,               30
Then following close in silence for—for what?
'No rabbit, never fear, she ever got,
Yet always hunts. Today she nearly had one:
She would and she wouldn't. 'Twas like that. The bad one!
She's not much use, but still she's company,             35
Though I'm not. She goes everywhere with me.
So Alton I must reach tonight somehow:
I'll get no shakedown with that bedfellow
From farmers. Many a man sleeps worse tonight
Than I shall.' 'In the trenches.' 'Yes, that's right.    40
But they'll be out of that—I hope they be—
This weather, marching after the enemy.'
'And so I hope. Good luck.' And there I nodded
'Good-night. You keep straight on.' Stiffly he plodded;
And at his heels the crisp leaves scurried fast,         45
And the leaf-coloured robin watched. They passed,
The robin till next day, the man for good,
Together in the twilight of the wood.

## 30

### *Beauty*

What does it mean? Tired, angry, and ill at ease,
No man, woman, or child, alive could please
Me now. And yet I almost dare to laugh
Because I sit and frame an epitaph—
'Here lies all that no one loved of him                    5
And that loved no one.' Then in a trice that whim
Has wearied. But, though I am like a river
At fall of evening while it seems that never
Has the sun lighted it or warmed it, while
Cross breezes cut the surface to a file,                   10
This heart, some fraction of me, happily
Floats through the window even now to a tree
Down in the misting, dim-lit, quiet vale,
Not like a pewit that returns to wail
For something it has lost, but like a dove                 15
That slants unswerving to its home and love.
There I find my rest, as through the dusk air
Flies what yet lives in me: Beauty is there.

## 31

### [*The Gypsy*]

A fortnight before Christmas Gypsies were everywhere:
Vans were drawn up on wastes, women trailed to the fair.
'My gentleman,' said one, 'You've got a lucky face.'
'And you've a luckier,' I thought, 'if such a grace
And impudence in rags are lucky.' 'Give a penny            5
For the poor baby's sake.' 'Indeed I have not any
Unless you can give change for a sovereign, my dear.'
'Then just half a pipeful of tobacco can you spare?'

I gave it. With that much victory she laughed content.
I should have given more, but off and away she went          10
With her baby and her pink sham flowers to rejoin
The rest before I could translate to its proper coin
Gratitude for her grace. And I paid nothing then,
As I pay nothing now with the dipping of my pen
For her brother's music when he drummed the tambourine       15
And stamped his feet, which made the workmen passing grin,
While his mouth-organ changed to a rascally Bacchanal dance
'Over the hills and far away'. This and his glance
Outlasted all the fair, farmer and auctioneer,
Cheap-jack, balloon-man, drover with crooked stick, and steer,   20
Pig, turkey, goose, and duck, Christmas Corpses to be.
Not even the kneeling ox had eyes like the Romany.
That night he peopled for me the hollow wooded land,
More dark and wild than stormiest heavens, that I searched
    and scanned
Like a ghost new-arrived. The gradations of the dark          25
Were like an underworld of death, but for the spark
In the Gypsy boy's black eyes as he played and stamped his
    tune,
'Over the hills and far away', and a crescent moon.


32

## [*Ambition*]


Unless it was that day I never knew
Ambition. After a night of frost, before
The March sun brightened and the South-west blew,
Jackdaws began to shout and float and soar
Already, and one was racing straight and high          5
Alone, shouting like a black warrior
Challenges and menaces to the wide sky.
With loud long laughter then a woodpecker
Ridiculed the sadness of the owl's last cry.
And through the valley where all the folk astir          10

Made only plumes of pearly smoke to tower
Over dark trees and white meadows happier
Than was Elysium in that happy hour,
A train that roared along raised after it
And carried with it a motionless white bower 15
Of purest cloud, from end to end close-knit,
So fair it touched the roar with silence. Time
Was powerless while that lasted. I could sit
And think I had made the loveliness of prime,
Breathed its life into it and were its lord, 20
And no mind lived save this 'twixt clouds and rime.
Omnipotent I was, nor even deplored
That I did nothing. But the end fell like a bell:
The bower was scattered; far off the train roared.
But if this was ambition I cannot tell: 25
What 'twas ambition for I know not well.


# 33

## *House and Man*


One hour: as dim he and his house now look
As a reflection in a rippling brook,
While I remember him; but first, his house.
Empty it sounded. 'Twas dark with forest boughs
That brushed the walls and made the mossy tiles 5
Part of the squirrels' track. In all those miles
Of forest silence and forest murmur, only
One house—'Lonely,' he said, 'I wish it were lonely'—
Which the trees looked upon from every side,
And that was his.

          He waved good-bye to hide 10
A sigh that he converted to a laugh.
He seemed to hang rather than stand there, half
Ghost-like, half a beggar's rag, clean wrung
And useless on the briar where it has hung

Long years a-washing by sun and wind and rain.     15
But why I call back man and house again
Is that now on a beech-tree's tip I see
As then I saw—I at the gate, and he
In the house darkness,—a magpie veering about,
A magpie like a weathercock in doubt.     20


# 34

## *Parting*


The Past is a strange land, most strange.
Wind blows not there, nor does rain fall:
If they do, they cannot hurt at all.
Men of all kinds as equals range

The soundless fields and streets of it.     5
Pleasure and pain there have no sting,
The perished self not suffering
That lacks all blood and nerve and wit,

And is in shadow-land a shade.
Remembered joy and misery     10
Bring joy to the joyous equally;
Both sadden the sad. So memory made

Parting today a double pain:
First because it was parting; next
Because the ill it ended vexed     15
And mocked me from the Past again,

Not as what had been remedied
Had I gone on,—not that, oh no!
But as itself no longer woe;
Sighs, angry word and look and deed     20

Being faded: rather a kind of bliss,
For there spiritualized it lay
In the perpetual yesterday
That naught can stir or stain, like this.


## 35

### *First known when lost*

I never had noticed it until
'Twas gone,—the narrow copse
Where now the woodman lops
The last of the willows with his bill.

It was not more than a hedge o'ergrown.          5
One meadow's breadth away
I passed it day by day.
Now the soil is bare as a bone,

And black betwixt two meadows green,
Though fresh-cut faggot ends          10
Of hazel make some amends
With a gleam as if flowers they had been.

Strange it could have hidden so near!
And now I see as I look
That the small winding brook,          15
A tributary's tributary rises there.


## 36

### *May 23*

There never was a finer day,
And never will be while May is May,—

The third, and not the last of its kind;
But though fair and clear the two behind
Seemed pursued by tempests overpast;                    5
And the morrow with fear that it could not last
Was spoiled. Today ere the stones were warm
Five minutes of thunderstorm
Dashed it with rain, as if to secure,
By one tear, its beauty the luck to endure.             10

At midday then along the lane
Old Jack Noman appeared again,
Jaunty and old, crooked and tall,
And stopped and grinned at me over the wall,
With a cowslip bunch in his button-hole                 15
And one in his cap. Who could say if his roll
Came from flints in the road, the weather, or ale?
He was welcome as the nightingale.
Not an hour of the sun had been wasted on Jack.
'I've got my Indian complexion back'                    20
Said he. He was tanned like a harvester,
Like his short clay pipe, like the leaf and bur
That clung to his coat from last night's bed,
Like the ploughland crumbling red.
Fairer flowers were none on the earth                   25
Than his cowslips wet with the dew of their birth,
Or fresher leaves than the cress in his basket.
'Where did they come from, Jack?' 'Don't ask it,
And you'll be told no lies.' 'Very well:
Then I can't buy.' 'I don't want to sell.               30
Take them and these flowers, too, free.
Perhaps you have something to give me?
Wait till next time. The better the day . . .
The Lord couldn't make a better, I say;
If he could, he never has done.'                        35
So off went Jack with his roll-walk-run,
Leaving his cresses from Oakshott rill
And his cowslips from Wheatham hill.

'Twas the first day that the midges bit;
But though they bit me, I was glad of it:
Of the dust in my face, too, I was glad.
Spring could do nothing to make me sad.
Bluebells hid all the ruts in the copse.
The elm seeds lay in the road like hops,
That fine day, May the twenty-third,
The day Jack Noman disappeared.

40

45

# 37

## *The Barn*

They should never have built a barn there, at all—
Drip, drip, drip!—under that elm tree,
Though then it was young. Now it is old
But good, not like the barn and me.

Tomorrow they cut it down. They will leave
The barn, as I shall be left, maybe.
What holds it up? 'Twould not pay to pull down.
Well, this place has no other antiquity.

5

No abbey or castle looks so old
As this that Job Knight built in '54,
Built to keep corn for rats and men.
Now there's fowls in the roof, pigs on the floor.

10

What thatch survives is dung for the grass,
The best grass on the farm. A pity the roof
Will not bear a mower to mow it. But
Only fowls have foothold enough.

15

Starlings used to sit there with bubbling throats
Making a spiky beard as they chattered
And whistled and kissed, with heads in air,
Till they thought of something else that mattered.

20

But now they cannot find a place,
Among all those holes, for a nest any more.
It's the turn of lesser things, I suppose.
Once I fancied 'twas starlings they built it for.

# 38

## *Home* [1]

Not the end: but there's nothing more.
Sweet Summer and Winter rude
I have loved, and friendship and love,
The crowd and solitude:

But I know them: I weary not;                     5
But all that they mean I know.
I would go back again home
Now. Yet how should I go?

This is my grief. That land,
My home, I have never seen;                       10
No traveller tells of it,
However far he has been.

And could I discover it,
I fear my happiness there,
Or my pain, might be dreams of return            15
Here, to these things that were.

Remembering ills, though slight
Yet irremediable,
Brings a worse, an impurer pang
Than remembering what was well.                   20

No: I cannot go back,
And would not if I could.
Until blindness come, I must wait
And blink at what is not good.

## 39

## *The Owl*

Downhill I came, hungry, and yet not starved;
Cold, yet had heat within me that was proof
Against the North wind; tired, yet so that rest
Had seemed the sweetest thing under a roof.

Then at the inn I had food, fire, and rest,                   5
Knowing how hungry, cold, and tired was I.
All of the night was quite barred out except
An owl's cry, a most melancholy cry

Shaken out long and clear upon the hill,
No merry note, nor cause of merriment,                   10
But one telling me plain what I escaped
And others could not, that night, as in I went.

And salted was my food, and my repose,
Salted and sobered, too, by the bird's voice
Speaking for all who lay under the stars,                   15
Soldiers and poor, unable to rejoice.

## 40

## *The Child on the Cliff*

Mother, the root of this little yellow flower
Among the stones has the taste of quinine.
Things are strange today on the cliff. The sun shines so bright,
And the grasshopper works at his sewing-machine
So hard. Here's one on my hand, mother, look;                   5
I lie so still. There's one on your book.

But I have something to tell more strange. So leave
Your book to the grasshopper, mother dear,—
Like a green knight in a dazzling market-place,—
And listen now. Can you hear what I hear          10
Far out? Now and then the foam there curls
And stretches a white arm out like a girl's.

Fishes and gulls ring no bells. There cannot be
A chapel or church between here and Devon,
With fishes or gulls ringing its bell,—hark.—      15
Somewhere under the sea or up in heaven.
'It's the bell, my son, out in the bay
On the buoy. It does sound sweet today.'

Sweeter I never heard, mother, no, not in all Wales.
I should like to be lying under that foam,          20
Dead, but able to hear the sound of the bell,
And certain that you would often come
And rest, listening happily.
I should be happy if that could be.

41

## The Bridge

I have come a long way today:
On a strange bridge alone,
Remembering friends, old friends,
I rest, without smile or moan,
As they remember me without smile or moan.       5

All are behind, the kind
And the unkind too, no more
Tonight than a dream. The stream
Runs softly yet drowns the Past,
The dark-lit stream has drowned the Future and the Past.   10

No traveller has rest more blest
Than this moment brief between
Two lives, when the Night's first lights
And shades hide what has never been,
Things goodlier, lovelier, dearer, than will be or have been.    15


## 42

### *Good-night*

The skylarks are far behind that sang over the down;
I can hear no more those suburb nightingales;
Thrushes and blackbirds sing in the gardens of the town
In vain: the noise of man, beast, and machine prevails.

But the call of children in the unfamiliar streets        5
That echo with a familiar twilight echoing,
Sweet as the voice of nightingale or lark, completes
A magic of strange welcome, so that I seem a king

Among man, beast, machine, bird, child, and the ghost
That in the echo lives and with the echo dies.        10
The friendless town is friendly; homeless, I am not lost;
Though I know none of these doors, and meet but strangers' eyes.

Never again, perhaps, after tomorrow, shall
I see these homely streets, these church windows alight,
Not a man or woman or child among them all:        15
But it is All Friends' Night, a traveller's good night.


## 43

### *But these things also*

But these things also are Spring's—
On banks by the roadside the grass

Long-dead that is greyer now
Than all the Winter it was;

The shell of a little snail bleached                    5
In the grass; chip of flint, and mite
Of chalk; and the small birds' dung
In splashes of purest white:

All the white things a man mistakes
For earliest violets                                   10
Who seeks through Winter's ruins
Something to pay Winter's debts,

While the North blows, and starling flocks
By chattering on and on
Keep their spirits up in the mist,                     15
And Spring's here, Winter's not gone.


# 44

## The New House

Now first, as I shut the door,
I was alone
In the new house; and the wind
Began to moan.

Old at once was the house,                             5
And I was old;
My ears were teased with the dread
Of what was foretold,

Nights of storm, days of mist, without end;
Sad days when the sun                                  10
Shone in vain: old griefs, and griefs
Not yet begun.

All was foretold me; naught
Could I foresee;
But I learnt how the wind would sound          15
After these things should be.


# 45

## *The Barn and the Down*

It stood in the sunset sky
Like the straight-backed down,
Many a time—the barn
At the edge of the town,

So huge and dark that it seemed          5
It was the hill
Till the gable's precipice proved
It impossible.

Then the great down in the west
Grew into sight,          10
A barn stored full to the ridge
With black of night;

And the barn fell to a barn
Or even less
Before critical eyes and its own          15
Late mightiness.

But far down and near barn and I
Since then have smiled,
Having seen my new cautiousness
By itself beguiled          20

To disdain what seemed the barn
Till a few steps changed
It past all doubt to the down;
So the barn was avenged.

# 46

## *Sowing*

It was a perfect day
For sowing; just
As sweet and dry was the ground
As tobacco-dust.

I tasted deep the hour                                    5
Between the far
Owl's chuckling first soft cry
And the first star.

A long stretched hour it was;
Nothing undone                                          10
Remained; the early seeds
All safely sown.

And now, hark at the rain,
Windless and light,
Half a kiss, half a tear,                                15
Saying good-night.

# 47

## *March the 3rd*

Here again (she said) is March the third
And twelve hours singing for the bird
'Twixt dawn and dusk, from half past six
To half past six, never unheard.

'Tis Sunday, and the church-bells end                     5
With the birds' songs. I think they blend

45

Better than in the same fair days
That shall pronounce the Winter's end.

Do men mark, and none dares say,
How it may shift and long delay,                    10
Somewhere before the first of Spring,
But never fails, this singing day?

When it falls on Sunday, bells
Are a wild natural voice that dwells
On hillsides; but the birds' songs have          15
The holiness gone from the bells.

This day unpromised is more dear
Than all the named days of the year
When seasonable sweets come in,
Since now we know how lucky we are.               20


# 48

## *Two Pewits*

Under the after-sunset sky
Two pewits sport and cry,
More white than is the moon on high
Riding the dark surge silently;
More black than earth. Their cry                   5
Is the one sound under the sky.
They alone move, now low, now high,
And merrily they cry
To the mischievous Spring sky,
Plunging earthward, tossing high,                 10
Over the ghost who wonders why
So merrily they cry and fly,
Nor choose 'twixt earth and sky,
While the moon's quarter silently
Rides, and earth rests as silently.               15

## 49

### *Will you come?*

Will you come?
Will you come?
Will you ride
So late
At my side?                              5
O, will you come?

Will you come?
Will you come
If the night
Has a moon,                             10
Full and bright?
O, will you come?

Would you come?
Would you come
If the noon                             15
Gave light,
Not the moon?
Beautiful, would you come?

Would you have come?
Would you have come                     20
Without scorning,
Had it been
Still morning?
Beloved, would you have come?

If you come                             25
Haste and come.
Owls have cried;
It grows dark
To ride.
Beloved, beautiful, come.               30

50

## The Path

Running along a bank, a parapet
That saves from the precipitous wood below
The level road, there is a path. It serves
Children for looking down the long smooth steep,
Between the legs of beech and yew, to where                5
A fallen tree checks the sight: while men and women
Content themselves with the road and what they see
Over the bank, and what the children tell.
The path, winding like silver, trickles on,
Bordered and even invaded by thinnest moss               10
That tries to cover roots and crumbling chalk
With gold, olive, and emerald, but in vain.
The children wear it. They have flattened the bank
On top, and silvered it between the moss
With the current of their feet, year after year.          15
But the road is houseless, and leads not to school.
To see a child is rare there, and the eye
Has but the road, the wood that overhangs
And underyawns it, and the path that looks
As if it led on to some legendary                         20
Or fancied place where men have wished to go
And stay; till, sudden, it ends where the wood ends.

51

## [The Wasp Trap]

This moonlight makes
The lovely lovelier
Than ever before lakes
And meadows were.

And yet they are not,                                    5
Though this their hour is, more
Lovely than things that were not
Lovely before.

Nothing on earth,
And in the heavens no star,                             10
For pure brightness is worth
More than that jar,

For wasps meant, now
A star—long may it swing
From the dead apple-bough,                              15
So glistening.


## 52

### *A Tale* [Cancelled version]

There once the walls
Of the ruined cottage stood.
The periwinkle crawls
With flowers in its hair into the wood.

In flowerless hours                                      5
Never will the bank fail,
With everlasting flowers
On fragments of blue plates, to tell the tale.


## 53

### [*A Tale*] [Revised version]

Here once flint walls,
Pump, orchard and wood pile stood.

Blue periwinkle crawls
From the lost garden down into the wood.

The flowerless hours 5
Of Winter cannot prevail
To blight these other flowers,
Blue china fragments scattered, that tell the tale.


## 54

## *Wind and Mist*

They met inside the gateway that gives the view,
A hollow land as vast as heaven. 'It is
A pleasant day, sir.' 'A very pleasant day.'
'And what a view here. If you like angled fields
Of grass and grain bounded by oak and thorn, 5
Here is a league. Had we with Germany
To play upon this board it could not be
More dear than April has made it with a smile.
The fields beyond that league close in together
And merge, even as our days into the past, 10
Into one wood that has a shining pane
Of water. Then the hills of the horizon—
That is how I should make hills had I to show
One who would never see them what hills were like.'
'Yes. Sixty miles of South Downs at one glance. 15
Sometimes a man feels proud at them, as if
He had just created them with one mighty thought.'
'That house, though modern, could not be better planned
For its position. I never liked a new
House better. Could you tell me who lives in it?' 20
'No one.' 'Ah—and I was peopling all
Those windows on the south with happy eyes,
The terrace under them with happy feet;
Girls—' 'Sir, I know. I know. I have seen that house
Through mist look lovely as a castle in Spain, 25

And airier. I have thought: "'Twere happy there
To live." And I have laughed at that
Because I lived there then.' 'Extraordinary.'
'Yes, with my furniture and family
Still in it, I, knowing every nook of it                    30
And loving none, and in fact hating it.'
'Dear me! How could that be? But pardon me.'
'No offence. Doubtless the house was not to blame,
But the eye watching from those windows saw,
Many a day, day after day, mist—mist                       35
Like chaos surging back—and felt itself
Alone in all the world, marooned alone.
We lived in clouds, on a cliff's edge almost
(You see), and if clouds went, the visible earth
Lay too far off beneath and like a cloud.                  40
I did not know it was the earth I loved
Until I tried to live there in the clouds
And the earth turned to cloud.'
                              'You had a garden
Of flint and clay, too.' 'True; that was real enough.
The flint was the one crop that never failed.             45
The clay first broke my heart, and then my back;
And the back heals not. There were other things
Real, too. In that room at the gable a child
Was born while the wind chilled a summer dawn:
Never looked grey mind on a greyer one                     50
Than when the child's cry broke above the groans.'
'I hope they were both spared.' 'They were. Oh yes.
But flint and clay and childbirth were too real
For this cloud castle. I had forgot the wind.
Pray do not let me get on to the wind.                     55
You would not understand about the wind.
It is my subject, and compared with me
Those who have always lived on the firm ground
Are quite unreal in this matter of the wind.
There were whole days and nights when the wind and I       60
Between us shared the world, and the wind ruled
And I obeyed it and forgot the mist.
My past and the past of the world were in the wind.

Now you will say that though you understand
And feel for me, and so on, you yourself                        65
Would find it different. You are all like that
If once you stand here free from wind and mist:
I might as well be talking to wind and mist.
You would believe the house-agent's young man
Who gives no heed to anything I say.                            70
Good morning. But one word. I want to admit
That I would try the house once more, if I could;
As I should like to try being young again.'


# 55

## *A Gentleman*

'He has robbed two clubs. The judge at Salisbury
Can't give him more than he undoubtedly
Deserves. The scoundrel! Look at his photograph!
A lady-killer! Hanging's too good by half
For such as he.' So said the stranger, one            5
With crimes yet undiscovered or undone.
But at the inn the Gypsy dame began:
'Now he was what I call a gentleman.
He went along with Carrie, and when she
Had a baby he paid up so readily             10
His half a crown. Just like him. A crown'd have been
More like him. For I never knew him mean.
Oh! but he was such a nice gentleman. Oh!
Last time we met he said if me and Joe
Was anywhere near we must be sure and call.          15
He put his arms around our Amos all
As if he were his own son. I pray God
Save him from justice! Nicer man never trod.'

## 56

### *Lob*

At hawthorn-time in Wiltshire travelling
In search of something chance would never bring,
An old man's face, by life and weather cut
And coloured,—rough, brown, sweet as any nut,—
A land face, sea-blue-eyed,—hung in my mind       5
When I had left him many a mile behind.
All he said was: 'Nobody can't stop 'ee. It's
A footpath, right enough. You see those bits
Of mounds—that's where they opened up the barrows
Sixty years since, while I was scaring sparrows.    10
They thought as there was something to find there,
But couldn't find it, by digging, anywhere.'

To turn back then and seek him, where was the use?
There were three Manningfords,—Abbots, Bohun, and Bruce:
And whether Alton, not Manningford, it was          15
My memory could not decide, because
There was both Alton Barnes and Alton Priors.
All had their churches, graveyards, farms, and byres,
Lurking to one side up the paths and lanes,
Seldom well seen except by aeroplanes;              20
And when bells rang, or pigs squealed, or cocks crowed,
Then only heard. Ages ago the road
Approached. The people stood and looked and turned,
Nor asked it to come nearer, nor yet learned
To move out there and dwell in all men's dust.      25
And yet withal they shot the weathercock, just
Because 'twas he crowed out of tune, they said:
So now the copper weathercock is dead.
If they had reaped their dandelions and sold
Them fairly, they could have afforded gold.         30

Many years passed, and I went back again
Among those villages, and I looked for men
Who might have known my ancient. He himself
Had long been dead or laid upon the shelf,
I thought. One man I asked about him roared                              35
At my description: ' 'Tis old Bottlesford
He means, Bill.' But another said: 'Of course,
It was Jack Button up at the White Horse.
He's dead, sir, these three years.' This lasted till
A girl proposed Walker of Walker's Hill,                                 40
'Old Adam Walker. Adam's Point you'll see
Marked on the maps.'


                   'That was her roguery'
The next man said. He was a squire's son
Who loved wild bird and beast, and dog and gun
For killing them. He had loved them from his birth,                     45
One with another, as he loved the earth.
'The man may be like Button, or Walker, or
Like Bottlesford, that you want, but far more
He sounds like one I saw when I was a child.
I could almost swear to him. The man was wild                           50
And wandered. His home was where he was free.
Everybody has met one such man as he.
Does he keep clear old paths that no one uses
But once a life-time when he loves or muses?
He is English as this gate, these flowers, this mire.                   55
And when at eight years old Lob-lie-by-the-fire
Came in my books, this was the man I saw.
He has been in England as long as dove and daw,
Calling the wild cherry tree the merry tree,
The rose campion Bridget-in-her-bravery;                                60
And in a tender mood he, as I guess,
Christened one flower Live-in-idleness,
And while he walked from Exeter to Leeds
One April called all cuckoo-flowers Milkmaids.
From him old herbal Gerard learnt, as a boy,                            65
To name wild clematis the Traveller's-joy.

Our blackbirds sang no English till his ear
Told him they called his Jan Toy "Pretty dear".
(She was Jan Toy the Lucky, who, having lost
A shilling, and found a penny loaf, rejoiced.)                        70
For reasons of his own to him the wren
Is Jenny Pooter. Before all other men
'Twas he first called the Hog's Back the Hog's Back.
That Mother Dunch's Buttocks should not lack
Their name was his care. He too could explain                        75
Totteridge and Totterdown and Juggler's Lane:
He knows, if anyone. Why Tumbling Bay,
Inland in Kent, is called so, he might say.

'But little he says compared with what he does.
If ever a sage troubles him he will buzz                             80
Like a beehive to conclude the tedious fray:
And the sage, who knows all languages, runs away.
Yet Lob has thirteen hundred names for a fool,
And though he never could spare time for school
To unteach what the fox so well expressed,                           85
On biting the cock's head off,—Quietness is best,—
He can talk quite as well as anyone
After his thinking is forgot and done.
He first of all told someone else's wife,
For a farthing she'd skin a flint and spoil a knife                  90
Worth sixpence skinning it. She heard him speak:
"She had a face as long as a wet week"
Said he, telling the tale in after years.
With blue smock and with gold rings in his ears,
Sometimes he is a pedlar, not too poor                               95
To keep his wit. This is tall Tom that bore
The logs in, and with Shakespeare in the hall
Once talked, when icicles hung by the wall.
As Herne the Hunter he has known hard times.
On sleepless nights he made up weather rhymes                        100
Which others spoilt. And, Hob, being then his name,
He kept the hog that thought the butcher came
To bring his breakfast. "You thought wrong" said Hob.
When there were kings in Kent this very Lob,

Whose sheep grew fat and he himself grew merry,        105
Wedded the king's daughter of Canterbury;
For he alone, unlike squire, lord, and king,
Watched a night by her without slumbering;
He kept both waking. When he was but a lad
He won a rich man's heiress, deaf, dumb, and sad,        110
By rousing her to laugh at him. He carried
His donkey on his back. So they were married.
And while he was a little cobbler's boy
He tricked the giant coming to destroy
Shrewsbury by flood. "And how far is it yet?"        115
The giant asked in passing. "I forget;
But see these shoes I've worn out on the road
And we're not there yet." He emptied out his load
Of shoes. The giant sighed, and dropped from his spade
The earth for damming Severn, and thus made        120
The Wrekin hill; and little Ercall hill
Rose where the giant scraped his boots. While still
So young, our Jack was chief of Gotham's sages.
But long before he could have been wise, ages
Earlier than this, while he grew thick and strong        125
And ate his bacon, or, at times, sang a song
And merely smelt it, as Jack the giant-killer
He made a name. He, too, ground up the miller,
The Yorkshireman who ground men's bones for flour.

'Do you believe Jack dead before his hour?        130
Or that his name is Walker, or Bottlesford,
Or Button, a mere clown, or squire, or lord?
The man you saw,—Lob-lie-by-the-fire, Jack Cade,
Jack Smith, Jack Moon, poor Jack of every trade,
Young Jack, or old Jack, or Jack What-d'ye-call,        135
Jack-in-the-hedge, or Robin-run-by-the-wall,
Robin Hood, Ragged Robin, lazy Bob,
One of the lords of No Man's Land, good Lob,—
Although he was seen dying at Waterloo,
Hastings, Agincourt, and Sedgmoor, too,—        140
Lives yet. He never will admit he is dead
Till millers cease to grind men's bones for bread,

Not till our weathercock crows once again
And I remove my house out of the lane
On to the road.' With this he disappeared                           145
In hazel and thorn tangled with old-man's-beard.
But one glimpse of his back, as there he stood,
Choosing his way, proved him of old Jack's blood,
Young Jack perhaps, and now a Wiltshireman
As he has oft been since his days began.                            150


# 57

## [*Digging* 1]

Today I think
Only with scents,—scents dead leaves yield,
And bracken, and wild carrot's seed,
And the square mustard field;

Odours that rise                                                      5
When the spade wounds the roots of tree,
Rose, currant, raspberry, or goutweed,
Rhubarb or celery;

The smoke's smell, too,
Flowing from where a bonfire burns                                   10
The dead, the waste, the dangerous,
And all to sweetness turns.

It is enough
To smell, to crumble the dark earth,
While the robin sings over again                                     15
Sad songs of Autumn mirth.

## 58

### *Lovers*

The two men in the road were taken aback.
The lovers came out shading their eyes from the sun,
And never was white so white, or black so black,
As her cheeks and hair. 'There are more things than one
A man might turn into a wood for, Jack,'                    5
Said George; Jack whispered: 'He has not got a gun.
It's a bit too much of a good thing, I say.
They are going the other road, look. And see her run.'—
She ran—'What a thing it is, this picking may.'

## 59

### *In Memoriam* [Easter 1915]

The flowers left thick at nightfall in the wood
This Eastertide call into mind the men,
Now far from home, who, with their sweethearts, should
Have gathered them and will do never again.

## 60

### *Head and Bottle*

The downs will lose the sun, white alyssum
Lose the bees' hum;
But head and bottle tilted back in the cart
Will never part
Till I am cold as midnight and all my hours          5
Are beeless flowers.

He neither sees, nor hears, nor smells, nor thinks,
But only drinks,
Quiet in the yard where tree trunks do not lie
More quietly.                                            10


61

*Home* [2]

Often I had gone this way before:
But now it seemed I never could be
And never had been anywhere else;
'Twas home; one nationality
We had, I and the birds that sang,              5
One memory.

They welcomed me. I had come back
That eve somehow from somewhere far:
The April mist, the chill, the calm,
Meant the same thing familiar                    10
And pleasant to us, and strange too,
Yet with no bar.

The thrush on the oak top in the lane
Sang his last song, or last but one;
And as he ended, on the elm                      15
Another had but just begun
His last; they knew no more than I
The day was done.

Then past his dark white cottage front
A labourer went along, his tread                 20
Slow, half with weariness half with ease;
And, through the silence, from his shed
The sound of sawing rounded all
That silence said.

## 62

## [*Health*]

Four miles at a leap, over the dark hollow land,
To the frosted steep of the down and its junipers black,
Travels my eye with equal ease and delight:
And scarce could my body leap four yards.

This is the best and the worst of it—          5
Never to know,
Yet to imagine gloriously, pure health.

Today, had I suddenly health,
I could not satisfy the desire of my heart
Unless health abated it,          10
So beautiful is the air in its softness and clearness, while Spring
Promises all and fails in nothing as yet;
And what blue and what white is I never knew
Before I saw this sky blessing the land.

For had I health I could not ride or run or fly          15
So far or so rapidly over the land
As I desire: I should reach Wiltshire tired;
I should have changed my mind before I could be in Wales.
I could not love; I could not command love.
Beauty would still be far off          20
However many hills I climbed over;
Peace would be still farther.
Maybe I should not count it anything
To leap these four miles with the eye;
And either I should not be filled almost to bursting with desire, 25
Or with my power desire would still keep pace.

Yet I am not satisfied
Even with knowing I never could be satisfied.
With health and all the power that lies
In maiden beauty, poet and warrior,          30
In Caesar, Shakespeare, Alcibiades,

Mazeppa, Leonardo, Michelangelo,
In any maiden whose smile is lovelier
Than sunlight upon dew,
I could not be as the wagtail running up and down          35
The warm tiles of the roof slope, twittering
Happily and sweetly as if the sun itself
Extracted the song
As the hand makes sparks from the fur of a cat:

I could not be as the sun.          40
Nor should I be content to be
As little as the bird or as mighty as the sun.
For the bird knows not of the sun,
And the sun regards not the bird.
But I am almost proud to love both bird and sun,          45
Though scarce this Spring could my body leap four yards.


# 63

## *The Huxter*

He has a hump like an ape on his back;
He has of money a plentiful lack;
And but for a gay coat of double his girth
There is not a plainer thing on the earth
    This fine May morning.          5

But the huxter has a bottle of beer;
He drives a cart and his wife sits near
Who does not heed his lack or his hump;
And they laugh as down the lane they bump
    This fine May morning.          10

# 64

## [*She dotes*]

She dotes on what the wild birds say
Or hint or mock at, night and day,—
Thrush, blackbird, all that sing in May,
     And songless plover,
Hawk, heron, owl, and woodpecker.     5
They never say a word to her
     About her lover.

She laughs at them for childishness,
She cries at them for carelessness
Who see her going loverless     10
     Yet sing and chatter
Just as when he was not a ghost,
Nor ever ask her what she has lost
     Or what is the matter.

Yet she has fancied blackbirds hide     15
A secret, and that thrushes chide
Because she thinks death can divide
     Her from her lover;
And she has slept, trying to translate
The word the cuckoo cries to his mate     20
     Over and over.

# 65

## *Song* [1]

She is beautiful
With happiness invincible:
If cruel she be
It is the hawk's proud innocent cruelty.

At poet's tears,                                               5
Sweeter than any smiles but hers,
She laughs; I sigh;
And yet I could not live if she should die.

And when in June
Once more the cuckoo spoils his tune,                         10
She laughs at sighs;
And yet she says she loves me till she dies.

# 66

## [*A Cat*]

She had a name among the children;
But no one loved though someone owned
Her, locked her out of doors at bedtime
And had her kittens duly drowned.

In Spring, nevertheless, this cat                             5
Ate blackbirds, thrushes, nightingales,
And birds of bright voice and plume and flight,
As well as scraps from neighbours' pails.

I loathed and hated her for this;
One speckle on a thrush's breast                              10
Was worth a million such; and yet
She lived long, till God gave her rest.

# 67

## *Melancholy*

The rain and wind, the rain and wind, raved endlessly.
On me the Summer storm, and fever, and melancholy
Wrought magic, so that if I feared the solitude
Far more I feared all company: too sharp, too rude,

Had been the wisest or the dearest human voice.                    5
What I desired I knew not, but whate'er my choice
Vain it must be, I knew. Yet naught did my despair
But sweeten the strange sweetness, while through the wild air
All day long I heard a distant cuckoo calling
And, soft as dulcimers, sounds of near water falling,             10
And, softer, and remote as if in history,
Rumours of what had touched my friends, my foes, or me.


# 68

## *Tonight*

Harry, you know at night
The larks in Castle Alley
Sing from the attic's height
As if the electric light
Were the true sun above a summer valley:            5
Whistle, don't knock, tonight.

I shall come early, Kate;
And we in Castle Alley
Will sit close out of sight
Alone, and ask no light                              10
Of lamp or sun above a summer valley:
Tonight I can stay late.


# 69

## *April*

The sweetest thing, I thought
At one time, between earth and heaven
Was the first smile
When mist has been forgiven

And the sun has stolen out,                                    5
Peered, and resolved to shine at seven
On dabbled lengthening grasses,
Thick primroses and early leaves uneven,
When earth's breath, warm and humid, far surpasses
The richest oven's, and loudly rings 'cuckoo'               10
And sharply the nightingale's 'tsoo, troo, tsoo, troo';
To say 'God bless it' was all that I could do.

But now I know one sweeter
By far since the day Emily
Turned weeping back                                             15
To me, still happy me,
To ask forgiveness,—
Yet smiled with half a certainty
To be forgiven,—for what
She had never done; I knew not what it might be,           20
Nor could she tell me, having now forgot,
By rapture carried with me past all care
As to an isle in April lovelier
Than April's self. 'God bless you' I said to her.


70

## The Glory

The glory of the beauty of the morning,—
The cuckoo crying over the untouched dew;
The blackbird that has found it, and the dove
That tempts me on to something sweeter than love;
White clouds ranged even and fair as new-mown hay;         5
The heat, the stir, the sublime vacancy
Of sky and meadow and forest and my own heart:—
The glory invites me, yet it leaves me scorning
All I can ever do, all I can be,
Beside the lovely of motion, shape, and hue,               10
The happiness I fancy fit to dwell

In beauty's presence. Shall I now this day
Begin to seek as far as heaven, as hell,
Wisdom or strength to match this beauty, start
And tread the pale dust pitted with small dark drops,        15
In hope to find whatever it is I seek,
Hearkening to short-lived happy-seeming things
That we know naught of, in the hazel copse?
Or must I be content with discontent
As larks and swallows are perhaps with wings?        20
And shall I ask at the day's end once more
What beauty is, and what I can have meant
By happiness? And shall I let all go,
Glad, weary, or both? Or shall I perhaps know
That I was happy oft and oft before,        25
Awhile forgetting how I am fast pent,
How dreary-swift, with naught to travel to,
Is Time? I cannot bite the day to the core.


71

### July


Naught moves but clouds, and in the glassy lake
Their doubles and the shadow of my boat.
The boat itself stirs only when I break
This drowse of heat and solitude afloat
To prove if what I see be bird or mote,        5
Or learn if yet the shore woods be awake.

Long hours since dawn grew,—spread,—and passed on high
And deep below,—I have watched the cool reeds hung
Over images more cool in imaged sky:
Nothing there was worth thinking of so long;        10
All that the ring-doves say, far leaves among,
Brims my mind with content thus still to lie.

72

## *The Chalk Pit*

'Is this the road that climbs above and bends
Round what was once a chalk pit: now it is
By accident an amphitheatre.
Some ash trees standing ankle-deep in brier
And bramble act the parts, and neither speak          5
Nor stir.' 'But see: they have fallen, every one,
And brier and bramble have grown over them.'
'That is the place. As usual no one is here.
Hardly can I imagine the drop of the axe,
And the smack that is like an echo, sounding here.'    10
'I do not understand.' 'Why, what I mean is
That I have seen the place two or three times
At most, and that its emptiness and silence
And stillness haunt me, as if just before
It was not empty, silent, still, but full              15
Of life of some kind, perhaps tragical.
Has anything unusual happened here?'

'Not that I know of. It is called the Dell.
They have not dug chalk here for a century.
That was the ash trees' age. But I will ask.'          20
'No. Do not. I prefer to make a tale,
Or better leave it like the end of a play,
Actors and audience and lights all gone;
For so it looks now. In my memory
Again and again I see it, strangely dark,              25
And vacant of a life but just withdrawn.
We have not seen the woodman with the axe.
Some ghost has left it now as we two came.'

'And yet you doubted if this were the road?'
'Well, sometimes I have thought of it and failed       30
To place it. No. And I am not quite sure,

Even now, this is it. For another place,
Real or painted, may have combined with it.
Or I myself a long way back in time . . .'
'Why, as to that, I used to meet a man—                    35
I had forgotten,—searching for birds' nests
Along the road and in the chalk pit too.
The wren's hole was an eye that looked at him
For recognition. Every nest he knew.
He got a stiff neck, by looking this side or that,         40
Spring after spring, he told me, with his laugh,—
A sort of laugh. He was a visitor,
A man of forty,—smoked and strolled about.
At orts and crosses Pleasure and Pain had played
On his brown features;—I think both had lost;—            45
Mild and yet wild too. You may know the kind.
And once or twice a woman shared his walks,
A girl of twenty with a brown boy's face,
And hair brown as a thrush or as a nut,
Thick eyebrows, glinting eyes—' 'You have said enough.     50
A pair,—free thought, free love,—I know the breed:
I shall not mix my fancies up with them.'

'You please yourself. I should prefer the truth
Or nothing. Here, in fact, is nothing at all
Except a silent place that once rang loud,                 55
And trees and us—imperfect friends, we men
And trees since time began; and nevertheless
Between us still we breed a mystery.'


# 73

## *Fifty Faggots*

There they stand, on their ends, the fifty faggots
That once were underwood of hazel and ash
In Jenny Pinks's Copse. Now, by the hedge
Close packed, they make a thicket fancy alone

Can creep through with the mouse and wren. Next Spring 5
A blackbird or a robin will nest there,
Accustomed to them, thinking they will remain
Whatever is for ever to a bird:
This Spring it is too late; the swift has come.
'Twas a hot day for carrying them up: 10
Better they will never warm me, though they must
Light several Winters' fires. Before they are done
The war will have ended, many other things
Have ended, maybe, that I can no more
Foresee or more control than robin and wren. 15


# 74

## *Sedge-Warblers* [Cancelled version]

This beauty made me dream there was a time
Long past and irrecoverable, a clime
Where any brook so radiant racing clear
Through buttercup and kingcup bright as brass
But gentle, nourishing the meadow grass 5
That leans and scurries in the wind, would bear
Another beauty, divine and feminine,
Child to the sun, a nymph whose soul unstained
Could love all day, and never hate or tire,
A lover of mortal or immortal kin. 10

And yet, rid of this dream, ere I had drained
Its poison, quieted was my desire
So that I only looked into the water,
Clearer than any goddess or man's daughter,
And hearkened while it combed the dark green hair 15
And shook the millions of the blossoms white
Of water-crowfoot, and curdled to one sheet
The flowers fallen from the chestnuts in the park
Far off. And sedge-warblers, clinging so light
To willow twigs, sang longer than the lark, 20

Quick, shrill, or grating, a song to match the heat
Of the strong sun, nor less the water's cool,
Gushing through narrows, swirling in the pool.
Their song that lacks all words, all melody,
All sweetness almost, was dearer then to me                    25
Than sweetest voice that sings in tune sweet words.
This was the best of May—the small brown birds
Wisely reiterating endlessly
What no man learnt yet, in or out of school.


# 75

## *Sedge-Warblers* [Revised version]

This beauty makes me dream there was a time
Long past and irrecoverable, a clime
Where river of such radiance racing clear
Through buttercup and kingcup bright as brass
But gentle, nourishing the meadowgrass                         5
That leans and scurries in the wind, would bear
Another beauty, divine and feminine,
Child of the sun, whose happy soul unstained
Could love all day, and never hate or tire,
Lover of mortal or immortal kin.                               10

And yet rid of this dream, ere I had drained
Its poison, quieted was my desire
So that I only looked into the water
And hearkened, while it combed the dark-green hair
And shook the millions of the blossoms white                  15
Of water crowfoot, and curdled in one sheet
The flowers fallen from the chestnuts in the park
Far off. The sedgewarblers that hung so light
On willow twigs, sang longer than any lark,
Quick, shrill or grating, a song to match the heat            20
Of the strong sun, nor less the water's cool
Gushing through narrows, swirling in the pool.

Their song that lacks all words, all melody,
All sweetness almost, was dearer now to me
Than sweetest voice that sings in tune sweet words:          25
This was the best of May, the small brown birds
Wisely reiterating endlessly
What no man learnt yet, in or out of school.

## 76

### [*I built myself a house of glass*]

I built myself a house of glass:
It took me years to make it:
And I was proud. But now, alas,
Would God someone would break it.

But it looks too magnificent.          5
No neighbour casts a stone
From where he dwells, in tenement
Or palace of glass, alone.

## 77

### *Words*

Out of us all
That make rhymes,
Will you choose
Sometimes—
As the winds use          5
A crack in a wall
Or a drain,
Their joy or their pain
To whistle through—
Choose me,          10
You English words?

I know you:
You are light as dreams,
Tough as oak,
Precious as gold,                                    15
As poppies and corn,
Or an old cloak:
Sweet as our birds
To the ear,
As the burnet rose                                   20
In the heat
Of Midsummer:
Strange as the races
Of dead and unborn:
Strange and sweet                                    25
Equally,
And familiar,
To the eye,
As the dearest faces
That a man knows,                                    30
And as lost homes are:
But though older far
Than oldest yew,—
As our hills are, old,—
Worn new                                             35
Again and again;
Young as our streams
After rain:
And as dear
As the earth which you prove                         40
That we love.

Make me content
With some sweetness
From Wales
Whose nightingales                                   45
Have no wings,—
From Wiltshire and Kent
And Herefordshire,
And the villages there,—

From the names, and the things          50
No less.

Let me sometimes dance
With you,
Or climb
Or stand perchance                       55
In ecstasy,
Fixed and free
In a rhyme,
As poets do.

# 78

## *The Word*

There are so many things I have forgot,
That once were much to me, or that were not,
All lost, as is a childless woman's child
And its child's children, in the undefiled
Abyss of what can never be again.             5
I have forgot, too, names of the mighty men
That fought and lost or won in the old wars,
Of kings and fiends and gods, and most of the stars.
Some things I have forgot that I forget.
But lesser things there are, remembered yet,   10
Than all the others. One name that I have not—
Though 'tis an empty thingless name—forgot
Never can die because Spring after Spring
Some thrushes learn to say it as they sing.
There is always one at midday saying it clear  15
And tart—the name, only the name I hear.
While perhaps I am thinking of the elder scent
That is like food, or while I am content
With the wild rose scent that is like memory,
This name suddenly is cried out to me           20
From somewhere in the bushes by a bird
Over and over again, a pure thrush word.

73

## 79

### *Under the Wood*

When these old woods were young
The thrushes' ancestors
As sweetly sung
In the old years.

There was no garden here,    5
Apples nor mistletoe;
No children dear
Ran to and fro.

New then was this thatched cot,
But the keeper was old,    10
And he had not
Much lead or gold.

Most silent beech and yew:
As he went round about
The woods to view    15
Seldom he shot.

But now that he is gone
Out of most memories,
Still lingers on
A stoat of his,    20

But one, shrivelled and green,
And with no scent at all,
And barely seen
On this shed wall.

## 80

## *Haymaking*

After night's thunder far away had rolled
The fiery day had a kernel sweet of cold,
And in the perfect blue the clouds uncurled,
Like the first gods before they made the world
And misery, swimming the stormless sea                    5
In beauty and in divine gaiety.
The smooth white empty road was lightly strewn
With leaves—the holly's Autumn falls in June—
And fir cones standing stiff up in the heat.
The mill-foot water tumbled white and lit                 10
With tossing crystals, happier than any crowd
Of children pouring out of school aloud.
And in the little thickets where a sleeper
For ever might lie lost, the nettle-creeper
And garden warbler sang unceasingly;                      15
While over them shrill shrieked in his fierce glee
The swift with wings and tail as sharp and narrow
As if the bow had flown off with the arrow.
Only the scent of woodbine and hay new-mown
Travelled the road. In the field sloping down,            20
Park-like, to where its willows showed the brook,
Haymakers rested. The tosser lay forsook
Out in the sun; and the long waggon stood
Without its team; it seemed it never would
Move from the shadow of that single yew.                  25
The team, as still, until their task was due,
Beside the labourers enjoyed the shade
That three squat oaks mid-field together made
Upon a circle of grass and weed uncut,
And on the hollow, once a chalk-pit, but                  30
Now brimmed with nut and elder-flower so clean.
The men leaned on their rakes, about to begin,

But still. And all were silent. All was old,
This morning time, with a great age untold,
Older than Clare and Cowper, Morland and Crome,     35
Than, at the field's far edge, the farmer's home,
A white house crouched at the foot of a great tree.
Under the heavens that know not what years be
The men, the beasts, the trees, the implements
Uttered even what they will in times far hence—     40
All of us gone out of the reach of change—
Immortal in a picture of an old grange.


# 81

## *A Dream* [*Sonnet* 1]

Over known fields with an old friend in dream *a*
I walked, but came sudden to a strange stream. *a*
Its dark waters were bursting out most bright *b*
From a great mountain's heart into the light. *b*
They ran a short course under the sun, then back *c*     5
Into a pit they plunged, once more as black *c*
As at their birth: and I stood thinking there *d*
How white, had the day shone on them, they were, *d*
Heaving and coiling. So by the roar and hiss *e*
And by the mighty motion of the abyss *e*     10
I was bemused, that I forgot my friend *f*
And neither saw nor sought him till the end, *f*
When I awoke from waters unto men *g*
Saying: 'I shall be here some day again.' *g*


# 82

## *The Brook*

Seated once by a brook, watching a child
Chiefly that paddled, I was thus beguiled.

Mellow the blackbird sang and sharp the thrush
Not far off in the oak and hazel brush,
Unseen. There was a scent like honeycomb                    5
From mugwort dull. And down upon the dome
Of the stone the cart-horse kicks against so oft
A butterfly alighted. From aloft
He took the heat of the sun, and from below.
On the hot stone he perched contented so,                   10
As if never a cart would pass again
That way; as if I were the last of men
And he the first of insects to have earth
And sun together and to know their worth.
I was divided between him and the gleam,                    15
The motion, and the voices, of the stream,
The waters running frizzled over gravel,
That never vanish and for ever travel.
A grey flycatcher silent on a fence
And I sat as if we had been there since                     20
The horseman and the horse lying beneath
The fir-tree-covered barrow on the heath,
The horseman and the horse with silver shoes,
Galloped the downs last. All that I could lose
I lost. And then the child's voice raised the dead.         25
'No one's been here before' was what she said
And what I felt, yet never should have found
A word for, while I gathered sight and sound.


# 83

## *Aspens*


All day and night, save winter, every weather,
Above the inn, the smithy, and the shop,
The aspens at the cross-roads talk together
Of rain, until their last leaves fall from the top.

Out of the blacksmith's cavern comes the ringing 5
Of hammer, shoe, and anvil; out of the inn
The clink, the hum, the roar, the random singing—
The sounds that for these fifty years have been.

The whisper of the aspens is not drowned,
And over lightless pane and footless road, 10
Empty as sky, with every other sound
Not ceasing, calls their ghosts from their abode,

A silent smithy, a silent inn, nor fails
In the bare moonlight or the thick-furred gloom,
In tempest or the night of nightingales, 15
To turn the cross-roads to a ghostly room.

And it would be the same were no house near.
Over all sorts of weather, men, and times,
Aspens must shake their leaves and men may hear
But need not listen, more than to my rhymes. 20

Whatever wind blows, while they and I have leaves
We cannot other than an aspen be
That ceaselessly, unreasonably grieves,
Or so men think who like a different tree.

# 84

## *The Mill-Water*

Only the sound remains
Of the old mill;
Gone is the wheel;
On the prone roof and walls the nettle reigns.

Water that toils no more 5
Dangles white locks
And, falling, mocks
The music of the mill-wheel's busy roar.

Pretty to see, by day
Its sound is naught                                    10
Compared with thought
And talk and noise of labour and of play.

Night makes the difference.
In calm moonlight,
Gloom infinite,                                        15
The sound comes surging in upon the sense:

Solitude, company,—
When it is night,—
Grief or delight
By it must haunted or concluded be.                    20

Often the silentness
Has but this one
Companion;
Wherever one creeps in the other is:

Sometimes a thought is drowned                         25
By it, sometimes
Out of it climbs;
All thoughts begin or end upon this sound,

Only the idle foam
Of water falling                                       30
Changelessly calling,
Where once men had a work-place and a home.

## 85

### *For these [Prayer]*

An acre of land between the shore and the hills,
Upon a ledge that shows my kingdoms three,
The lovely visible earth and sky and sea,
Where what the curlew needs not, the farmer tills:

A house that shall love me as I love it,                      5
Well-hedged, and honoured by a few ash-trees
That linnets, greenfinches, and goldfinches
Shall often visit and make love in and flit:

A garden I need never go beyond,
Broken but neat, whose sunflowers every one              10
Are fit to be the sign of the Rising Sun:
A spring, a brook's bend, or at least a pond:

For these I ask not, but, neither too late
Nor yet too early, for what men call content,
And also that something may be sent                         15
To be contented with, I ask of fate.


# 86

## *Digging* [2]

What matter makes my spade for tears or mirth,
Letting down two clay pipes into the earth?
The one I smoked, the other a soldier
Of Blenheim, Ramillies, and Malplaquet
Perhaps. The dead man's immortality                         5
Lies represented lightly with my own,
A yard or two nearer the living air
Than bones of ancients who, amazed to see
Almighty God erect the mastodon,
Once laughed, or wept, in this same light of day.          10


# 87

## *Two Houses*

Between a sunny bank and the sun
The farmhouse smiles

On the riverside plat:
No other one
So pleasant to look at                                    5
And remember, for many miles,
So velvet-hushed and cool under warm tiles.

Nor far from the road it lies, yet caught
Far out of reach
Of the road's dust                                       10
And the dusty thought
Of passers-by, though each
Stops, and turns, and must
Look down at it like a wasp at a muslined peach.

But another house stood there long before:               15
And as if above graves
Still the turf heaves
Above its stones:
Dark hangs the sycamore,
Shadowing kennel and bones                               20
And the black dog that shakes his chain and moans.

And when he barks, over the river
Flashing fast,
Dark echoes reply,
And the hollow past                                      25
Half yields the dead that never
More than half hidden lie:
And out they creep and back again for ever.

# 88

## *Cock-Crow*

Out of the wood of thoughts that grows by night
To be cut down by the sharp axe of light,—
Out of the night, two cocks together crow,

Cleaving the darkness with a silver blow:
And bright before my eyes twin trumpeters stand,      5
Heralds of splendour, one at either hand,
Each facing each as in a coat of arms:
The milkers lace their boots up at the farms.

# 89

## *October*

The green elm with the one great bough of gold
Lets leaves into the grass slip, one by one.—
The short hill grass, the mushrooms small milk-white,
Harebell and scabious and tormentil,
That blackberry and gorse, in dew and sun,      5
Bow down to; and the wind travels too light
To shake the fallen birch leaves from the fern;
The gossamers wander at their own will.
At heavier steps than birds' the squirrels scold.

The late year has grown fresh again and new      10
As Spring, and to the touch is not more cool
Than it is warm to the gaze; and now I might
As happy be as earth is beautiful,
Were I some other or with earth could turn
In alternation of violet and rose,      15
Harebell and snowdrop, at their season due,
And gorse that has no time not to be gay.
But if this be not happiness, who knows?
Some day I shall think this a happy day,
And this mood by the name of melancholy      20
Shall no more blackened and obscured be.

## 90

### *There's nothing like the sun*

There's nothing like the sun as the year dies,
Kind as it can be, this world being made so,
To stones and men and beasts and birds and flies,
To all things that it touches except snow,
Whether on mountain side or street of town.          5
The south wall warms me: November has begun,
Yet never shone the sun as fair as now
While the sweet last-left damsons from the bough
With spangles of the morning's storm drop down
Because the starling shakes it, whistling what          10
Once swallows sang. But I have not forgot
That there is nothing, too, like March's sun,
Like April's, or July's, or June's, or May's,
Or January's, or February's, great days:
And August, September, October, and December          15
Have equal days, all different from November.
No day of any month but I have said—
Or, if I could live long enough, should say—
'There's nothing like the sun that shines today.'
There's nothing like the sun till we are dead.          20

## 91

### *The Thrush*

When Winter's ahead,
What can you read in November
That you read in April
When Winter's dead?

I hear the thrush, and I see                    5
Him alone at the end of the lane
Near the bare poplar's tip,
Singing continuously.

Is it more that you know
Than that, even as in April,                    10
So in November,
Winter is gone that must go?

Or is all your lore
Not to call November November,
And April April,                                15
And Winter Winter—no more?

But I know the months all,
And their sweet names, April,
May and June and October,
As you call and call                            20

I must remember
What died into April
And consider what will be born
Of a fair November;

And April I love for what                       25
It was born of, and November
For what it will die in,
What they are and what they are not,

While you love what is kind,
What you can sing in                            30
And love and forget in
All that's ahead and behind.

## 92

## *Liberty*

The last light has gone out of the world, except
This moonlight lying on the grass like frost
Beyond the brink of the tall elm's shadow.
It is as if everything else had slept
Many an age, unforgotten and lost      5
The men that were, the things done, long ago,
All I have thought; and but the moon and I
Live yet and here stand idle over the grave
Where all is buried. Both have liberty
To dream what we could do if we were free      10
To do some thing we had desired long,
The moon and I. There's none less free than who
Does nothing and has nothing else to do,
Being free only for what is not to his mind,
And nothing is to his mind. If every hour      15
Like this one passing that I have spent among
The wiser others when I have forgot
To wonder whether I was free or not,
Were piled before me, and not lost behind,
And I could take and carry them away      20
I should be rich; or if I had the power
To wipe out every one and not again
Regret, I should be rich to be so poor.
And yet I still am half in love with pain,
With what is imperfect, with both tears and mirth,      25
With things that have an end, with life and earth,
And this moon that leaves me dark within the door.

## 93

### [*This is no case of petty right or wrong*]

This is no case of petty right or wrong
That politicians or philosophers
Can judge. I hate not Germans, nor grow hot
With love of Englishmen, to please newspapers.
Beside my hate for one fat patriot                        5
My hatred of the Kaiser is love true:—
A kind of god he is, banging a gong.
But I have not to choose between the two,
Or between justice and injustice. Dinned
With war and argument I read no more                     10
Than in the storm smoking along the wind
Athwart the wood. Two witches' cauldrons roar.
From one the weather shall rise clear and gay;
Out of the other an England beautiful
And like her mother that died yesterday.                 15
Little I know or care if, being dull,
I shall miss something that historians
Can rake out of the ashes when perchance
The phoenix broods serene above their ken.
But with the best and meanest Englishmen                 20
I am one in crying, God save England, lest
We lose what never slaves and cattle blessed.
The ages made her that made us from the dust:
She is all we know and live by, and we trust
She is good and must endure, loving her so:              25
And as we love ourselves we hate her foe.

## 94

### *Rain*

Rain, midnight rain, nothing but the wild rain
On this bleak hut, and solitude, and me
Remembering again that I shall die
And neither hear the rain nor give it thanks
For washing me cleaner than I have been                    5
Since I was born into this solitude.
Blessed are the dead that the rain rains upon:
But here I pray that none whom once I loved
Is dying tonight or lying still awake
Solitary, listening to the rain,                           10
Either in pain or thus in sympathy
Helpless among the living and the dead,
Like a cold water among broken reeds,
Myriads of broken reeds all still and stiff,
Like me who have no love which this wild rain             15
Has not dissolved except the love of death,
If love it be towards what is perfect and
Cannot, the tempest tells me, disappoint.

## 95

### *Song* [2]

The clouds that are so light,
Beautiful, swift and bright,
Cast shadows on field and park
Of the earth that is so dark,

And even so now, light one!                                        5
Beautiful, swift and bright one!
You let fall on a heart that was dark,
Unillumined, a deeper mark.

But clouds would have, without earth
To shadow, far less worth:                                        10
Away from your shadow on me
Your beauty less would be,

And if it still be treasured
An age hence, it shall be measured
By this small dark spot                                           15
Without which it were not.


## 96

### *Roads*

I love roads:
The goddesses that dwell
Far along invisible
Are my favourite gods.

Roads go on                                                       5
While we forget, and are
Forgotten like a star
That shoots and is gone.

On this earth 'tis sure
We men have not made                                             10
Anything that doth fade
So soon, so long endure:

The hill road wet with rain
In the sun would not gleam
Like a winding stream                              15
If we trod it not again.

They are lonely
While we sleep, lonelier
For lack of the traveller
Who is now a dream only.                           20

From dawn's twilight
And all the clouds like sheep
On the mountains of sleep
They wind into the night.

The next turn may reveal                           25
Heaven: upon the crest
The close pine clump, at rest
And black, may Hell conceal.

Often footsore, never
Yet of the road I weary,
Though long and steep and dreary                   30
As it winds on for ever.

Helen of the roads,
The mountain ways of Wales
And the Mabinogion tales,                          35
Is one of the true gods,

Abiding in the trees,
The threes and fours so wise,
The larger companies,
That by the roadside be,                           40

And beneath the rafter
Else uninhabited
Excepting by the dead;
And it is her laughter

At morn and night I hear                                           45
When the thrush cock sings
Bright irrelevant things,
And when the chanticleer

Calls back to their own night
Troops that make loneliness                                        50
With their light footsteps' press,
As Helen's own are light.

Now all roads lead to France
And heavy is the tread
Of the living; but the dead                                        55
Returning lightly dance:

Whatever the road bring
To me or take from me,
They keep me company
With their pattering,                                              60

Crowding the solitude
Of the loops over the downs,
Hushing the roar of towns
And their brief multitude.

# 97

## *The Ash Grove*

Half of the grove stood dead, and those that yet lived made
Little more than the dead ones made of shade.
If they led to a house, long before they had seen its fall:
But they welcomed me; I was glad without cause and delayed.

Scarce a hundred paces under the trees was the interval—    5
Paces each sweeter than sweetest miles—but nothing at all,
Not even the spirits of memory and fear with restless wing,
Could climb down in to molest me over the wall

That I passed through at either end without noticing.
And now an ash grove far from those hills can bring    10
The same tranquillity in which I wander a ghost
With a ghostly gladness, as if I heard a girl sing

The song of the Ash Grove soft as love uncrossed,
And then in a crowd or in distance it were lost,
But the moment unveiled something unwilling to die    15
And I had what most I desired, without search or desert or cost.

## 98

### *February Afternoon* [*Sonnet 2*]

Men heard this roar of parleying starlings, saw,
A thousand years ago even as now,
Black rooks with white gulls following the plough
So that the first are last until a caw
Commands that last are first again,—a law    5
Which was of old when one, like me, dreamed how
A thousand years might dust lie on his brow
Yet thus would birds do between hedge and shaw.

Time swims before me, making as a day
A thousand years, while the broad ploughland oak    10
Roars mill-like and men strike and bear the stroke
Of war as ever, audacious or resigned,
And God still sits aloft in the array
That we have wrought him, stone-deaf and stone-blind.

## 99

### [*P. H. T.*]

I may come near loving you
When you are dead
And there is nothing to do
And much to be said.

To repent that day will be          5
Impossible
For you, and vain for me
The truth to tell.

I shall be sorry for
Your impotence:                     10
You can do and undo no more
When you go hence,

Cannot even forgive
The funeral.
But not so long as you live         15
Can I love you at all.

## 100

### [*These things that poets said*]

These things that poets said
Of love seemed true to me
When I loved and I fed
On love and poetry equally.

But now I wish I knew          5
If theirs were love indeed,
Or if mine were the true
And theirs some other lovely weed:

For certainly not thus,
Then or thereafter, I          10
Loved ever. Between us
Decide, good Love, before I die.

Only, that once I loved
By this one argument
Is very plainly proved:          15
I, loving not, am different.

## 101

## [*M. E. T.*]

No one so much as you
Loves this my clay,
Or would lament as you
Its dying day.

You know me through and through          5
Though I have not told,
And though with what you know
You are not bold.

None ever was so fair
As I thought you:          10
Not a word can I bear
Spoken against you.

All that I ever did
For you seemed coarse
Compared with what I hid          15
Nor put in force.

Scarce my eyes dare meet you
Lest they should prove
I but respond to you
And do not love.                                              20

We look and understand,
We cannot speak
Except in trifles and
Words the most weak.

I at the most accept                                          25
Your love, regretting
That is all: I have kept
A helpless fretting

That I could not return
All that you gave                                             30
And could not ever burn
With the love you have,

Till sometimes it did seem
Better it were
Never to see you more                                         35
Than linger here

With only gratitude
Instead of love—
A pine in solitude
Cradling a dove.                                              40

## 102

## *The Unknown*

She is most fair,
And when they see her pass
The poets' ladies
Look no more in the glass
But after her.                                    5

On a bleak moor
Running under the moon
She lures a poet,
Once proud or happy, soon
Far from his door.                                10

Beside a train,
Because they saw her go,
Or failed to see her,
Travellers and watchers know
Another pain.                                     15

The simple lack
Of her is more to me
Than others' presence,
Whether life splendid be
Or utter black.                                   20

I have not seen,
I have no news of her;
I can tell only
She is not here, but there
She might have been.                              25

She is to be kissed
Only perhaps by me;
She may be seeking
Me and no other: she
May not exist.                                    30

95

103

## *Celandine*

Thinking of her had saddened me at first,
Until I saw the sun on the celandines lie
Redoubled, and she stood up like a flame,
A living thing, not what before I nursed,
The shadow I was growing to love almost,                    5
The phantom, not the creature with bright eye
That I had thought never to see, once lost.

She found the celandines of February
Always before us all. Her nature and name
Were like those flowers, and now immediately          10
For a short swift eternity back she came,
Beautiful, happy, simply as when she wore
Her brightest bloom among the winter hues
Of all the world; and I was happy too,
Seeing the blossoms and the maiden who                  15
Had seen them with me Februarys before,
Bending to them as in and out she trod
And laughed, with locks sweeping the mossy sod.

But this was a dream: the flowers were not true,
Until I stooped to pluck from the grass there          20
One of five petals and I smelt the juice
Which made me sigh, remembering she was no more,
Gone like a never perfectly recalled air.

104

## '*Home*' [3]

Fair was the morning, fair our tempers, and
We had seen nothing fairer than that land,

Though strange, and the untrodden snow that made
Wild of the tame, casting out all that was
Not wild and rustic and old; and we were glad.                    5

Fair too was afternoon, and first to pass
Were we that league of snow, next the north wind.

There was nothing to return for except need.
And yet we sang nor ever stopped for speed,
As we did often with the start behind.                            10
Faster still strode we when we came in sight
Of the cold roofs where we must spend the night.

Happy we had not been there, nor could be,
Though we had tasted sleep and food and fellowship
Together long.
                        'How quick' to someone's lip             15
The word came, 'will the beaten horse run home.'

The word 'home' raised a smile in us all three,
And one repeated it, smiling just so
That all knew what he meant and none would say.
Between three counties far apart that lay                         20
We were divided and looked strangely each
At the other, and we knew we were not friends
But fellows in a union that ends
With the necessity for it, as it ought.

Never a word was spoken, not a thought                            25
Was thought, of what the look meant with the word
'Home' as we walked and watched the sunset blurred.
And then to me the word, only the word,
'Homesick', as it were playfully occurred:
No more. If I should ever more admit                              30
Than the mere word I could not endure it
For a day longer: this captivity
Must somehow come to an end, else I should be
Another man, as often now I seem,
Or this life be only an evil dream.                               35

## 105

## *Thaw*

Over the land freckled with snow half-thawed
The speculating rooks at their nests cawed
And saw from elm-tops, delicate as flower of grass,
What we below could not see, Winter pass.

## Household Poems

## 106

## [1 *Bronwen*]

If I should ever by chance grow rich
I'll buy Codham, Cockridden, and Childerditch,
Roses, Pyrgo, and Lapwater,
And let them all to my elder daughter.
The rent I shall ask of her will be only          5
Each year's first violets, white and lonely,
The first primroses and orchises—
She must find them before I do, that is.
But if she finds a blossom on furze
Without rent they shall all for ever be hers,          10
Codham, Cockridden, and Childerditch,
Roses, Pyrgo and Lapwater,—
I shall give them all to my elder daughter.

107

## [2 *Merfyn*]

If I were to own this countryside
As far as a man in a day could ride,
And the Tyes were mine for giving or letting,—
Wingle Tye and Margaretting
Tye,—and Skreens, Gooshays, and Cockerells,          5
Shellow, Rochetts, Bandish, and Pickerells,
Martins, Lambkins, and Lillyputs,
Their copses, ponds, roads, and ruts,
Fields where plough-horses steam and plovers
Fling and whimper, hedges that lovers          10
Love, and orchards, shrubberies, walls
Where the sun untroubled by north wind falls,
And single trees where the thrush sings well
His proverbs untranslatable,
I would give them all to my son          15
If he would let me any one
For a song, a blackbird's song, at dawn.
He should have no more, till on my lawn
Never a one was left, because I
Had shot them to put them into a pie,—          20
His Essex blackbirds, every one,
And I was left old and alone.

Then unless I could pay, for rent, a song
As sweet as a blackbird's, and as long—
No more—he should have the house, not I:          25
Margaretting or Wingle Tye,
Or it might be Skreens, Gooshays, or Cockerells,
Shellow, Rochetts, Bandish, or Pickerells,
Martins, Lambkins, or Lillyputs,
Should be his till the cart tracks had no ruts.          30

108

## [3 *Myfanwy*]

What shall I give my daughter the younger
More than will keep her from cold and hunger?
I shall not give her anything.
If she shared South Weald and Havering,
Their acres, the two brooks running between,     5
Paine's Brook and Weald Brook,
With pewit, woodpecker, swan, and rook,
She would be no richer than the queen
Who once on a time sat in Havering Bower
Alone, with the shadows, pleasure and power.     10
She could do no more with Samarcand,
Or the mountains of a mountain land
And its far white house above cottages
Like Venus above the Pleiades.
Her small hands I would not cumber            15
With so many acres and their lumber,
But leave her Steep and her own world
And her spectacled self with hair uncurled,
Wanting a thousand little things
That time without contentment brings.          20

109

## [4 *Helen*]

And you, Helen, what should I give you?
So many things I would give you
Had I an infinite great store
Offered me and I stood before
To choose. I would give you youth,             5
All kinds of loveliness and truth,

A clear eye as good as mine,
Lands, waters, flowers, wine,
As many children as your heart
Might wish for, a far better art                    10
Than mine can be, all you have lost
Upon the travelling waters tossed,
Or given to me. If I could choose
Freely in that great treasure-house
Anything from any shelf,                            15
I would give you back yourself,
And power to discriminate
What you want and want it not too late,
Many fair days free from care
And heart to enjoy both foul and fair,             20
And myself, too, if I could find
Where it lay hidden and it proved kind.


# 110

## [*The Wind's Song*] [*Sonnet* 3]

Dull-thoughted, walking among the nunneries
Of many a myriad anemones
In the close copses, I grew weary of Spring
Till I emerged and in my wandering
I climbed the down up to a lone pine clump          5
Of six, the tallest dead, one a mere stump.
On one long stem, branchless and flayed and prone
I sat in the sun listening to the wind alone,
Thinking there could be no old song so sad
As the wind's song; but later none so glad          10
Could I remember as that same wind's song
All the time blowing the pine boughs among.
My heart that had been still as the dead tree
Awakened by the West wind was made free.

## III

### 'Go now'

Like the touch of rain she was
On a man's flesh and hair and eyes
When the joy of walking thus
Has taken him by surprise:

With the love of the storm he burns,                    5
He sings, he laughs, well I know how,
But forgets when he returns
As I shall not forget her 'Go now'.

Those two words shut a door
Between me and the blessed rain                          10
That was never shut before
And will not open again.


## 112

### When we two walked

When we two walked in Lent
We imagined that happiness
Was something different
And this was something less.

But happy were we to hide                               5
Our happiness, not as they were
Who acted in their pride
Juno and Jupiter:

For the gods in their jealousy
Murdered that wife and man,                          10
And we that were wise live free
To recall our happiness then.


# 113

## *Tall Nettles*

Tall nettles cover up, as they have done
These many springs, the rusty harrow, the plough
Long worn out, and the roller made of stone:
Only the elm butt tops the nettles now.

This corner of the farmyard I like most:             5
As well as any bloom upon a flower
I like the dust on the nettles, never lost
Except to prove the sweetness of a shower.


# 114

## [*The Watchers*]

By the ford at the town's edge
Horse and carter rest:
The carter smokes on the bridge
Watching the water press in swathes about his horse's chest.

From the inn one watches, too,                       5
In the room for visitors
That has no fire, but a view
And many cases of stuffed fish, vermin, and kingfishers.

## 115

### [*I never saw that land before*]

I never saw that land before,
And now can never see it again;
Yet, as if by acquaintance hoar
Endeared, by gladness and by pain,
Great was the affection that I bore                    5

To the valley and the river small,
The cattle, the grass, the bare ash trees,
The chickens from the farmsteads, all
Elm-hidden, and the tributaries
Descending at equal interval;                          10

The blackthorns down along the brook
With wounds yellow as crocuses
Where yesterday the labourer's hook
Had sliced them cleanly; and the breeze
That hinted all and nothing spoke.                     15

I neither expected anything
Nor yet remembered: but some goal
I touched then; and if I could sing
What would not even whisper my soul
As I went on my journeying,                            20

I should use, as the trees and birds did,
A language not to be betrayed;
And what was hid should still be hid
Excepting from those like me made
Who answer when such whispers bid.                     25

## 116

### *The Cherry Trees*

The cherry trees bend over and are shedding
On the old road where all that passed are dead,
Their petals, strewing the grass as for a wedding
This early May morn when there is none to wed.

## 117

### *It rains*

It rains, and nothing stirs within the fence
Anywhere through the orchard's untrodden, dense
Forest of parsley. The great diamonds
Of rain on the grassblades there is none to break,
Or the fallen petals further down to shake.                    5

And I am nearly as happy as possible
To search the wilderness in vain though well,
To think of two walking, kissing there,
Drenched, yet forgetting the kisses of the rain:
Sad, too, to think that never, never again,             10

Unless alone, so happy shall I walk
In the rain. When I turn away, on its fine stalk
Twilight has fined to naught, the parsley flower
Figures, suspended still and ghostly white,
The past hovering as it revisits the light.              15

## 118

### *Some eyes condemn [Sonnet 4]*

Some eyes condemn the earth they gaze upon:
Some wait patiently till they know far more
Than earth can tell them: some laugh at the whole
As folly of another's making: one
I knew that laughed because he saw, from core      5
To rind, not one thing worth the laugh his soul
Had ready at waking: some eyes have begun
With laughing; some stand startled at the door.

Others, too, I have seen rest, question, roll,
Dance, shoot. And many I have loved watching. Some   10
I could not take my eyes from till they turned
And loving died. I had not found my goal.
But thinking of your eyes, dear, I become
Dumb: for they flamed, and it was me they burned.

## 119

### *The sun used to shine*

The sun used to shine while we two walked
Slowly together, paused and started
Again, and sometimes mused, sometimes talked
As either pleased, and cheerfully parted

Each night. We never disagreed                    5
Which gate to rest on. The to be
And the late past we gave small heed.
We turned from men or poetry

To rumours of the war remote
Only till both stood disinclined                  10

For aught but the yellow flavorous coat
Of an apple wasps had undermined;

Or a sentry of dark betonies,
The stateliest of small flowers on earth,
At the forest verge; or crocuses              15
Pale purple as if they had their birth

In sunless Hades fields. The war
Came back to mind with the moonrise
Which soldiers in the east afar
Beheld then. Nevertheless, our eyes         20

Could as well imagine the Crusades
Or Caesar's battles. Everything
To faintness like those rumours fades—
Like the brook's water glittering

Under the moonlight—like those walks     25
Now—like us two that took them, and
The fallen apples, all the talks
And silences—like memory's sand

When the tide covers it late or soon,
And other men through other flowers     30
In those fields under the same moon
Go talking and have easy hours.

## 120

## [*Bugle Call*]

'No one cares less than I,
Nobody knows but God
Whether I am destined to lie
Under a foreign clod'
Were the words I made to the bugle call in the morning.    5

But laughing, storming, scorning,
Only the bugles know
What the bugles say in the morning,
And they do not care, when they blow
The call that I heard and made words to early this morning.      10

## 121

### *As the team's head brass*

As the team's head brass flashed out on the turn
The lovers disappeared into the wood.
I sat among the boughs of the fallen elm
That strewed an angle of the fallow, and
Watched the plough narrowing a yellow square      5
Of charlock. Every time the horses turned
Instead of treading me down, the ploughman leaned
Upon the handles to say or ask a word,
About the weather, next about the war.
Scraping the share he faced towards the wood,      10
And screwed along the furrow till the brass flashed
Once more.
          The blizzard felled the elm whose crest
I sat in, by a woodpecker's round hole,
The ploughman said. 'When will they take it away?'
'When the war's over.' So the talk began—      15
One minute and an interval of ten,
A minute more and the same interval.
'Have you been out?' 'No.' 'And don't want to, perhaps?'
'If I could only come back again, I should.
I could spare an arm. I shouldn't want to lose      20
A leg. If I should lose my head, why, so,
I should want nothing more. . . . Have many gone
From here?' 'Yes.' 'Many lost?' 'Yes, a good few.
Only two teams work on the farm this year.
One of my mates is dead. The second day      25
In France they killed him. It was back in March,

The very night of the blizzard, too. Now if
He had stayed here we should have moved the tree.'
'And I should not have sat here. Everything
Would have been different. For it would have been            30
Another world.' 'Ay, and a better, though
If we could see all all might seem good.' Then
The lovers came out of the wood again:
The horses started and for the last time
I watched the clods crumble and topple over            35
After the ploughshare and the stumbling team.


## 122

### *After you speak*


After you speak
And what you meant
Is plain,
My eyes
Meet yours that mean—            5
With your cheeks and hair—
Something more wise,
More dark,
And far different.
Even so the lark            10
Loves dust
And nestles in it
The minute
Before he must
Soar in lone flight            15
So far,
Like a black star
He seems—
A mote
Of singing dust            20
Afloat
Above,

That dreams
And sheds no light.
I know your lust                                          25
Is love.


## 123

## *The Pond*

Bright clouds of may
Shade half the pond.
Beyond,
All but one bay
Of emerald                                               5
Tall reeds
Like criss-cross bayonets
Where a bird once called,
Lies bright as the sun.
No one heeds.                                            10
The light wind frets
And drifts the scum
Of may-blossom.
Till the moorhen calls
Again                                                    15
Naught's to be done
By birds or men.
Still the may falls.


## 124

## [*Song* 3]

Early one morning in May I set out,
And nobody I knew was about.
    I'm bound away for ever,
     Away somewhere, away for ever.

There was no wind to trouble the weathercocks. 5
I had burnt my letters and darned my socks.

No one knew I was going away,
I thought myself I should come back some day.

I heard the brook through the town gardens run.
O sweet was the mud turned to dust by the sun. 10

A gate banged in a fence and banged in my head.
'A fine morning, sir,' a shepherd said.

I could not return from my liberty,
To my youth and my love and my misery.

The past is the only dead thing that smells sweet, 15
The only sweet thing that is not also fleet.
      I'm bound away for ever,
      Away somewhere, away for ever.


## 125

### *It was upon* [*Sonnet* 5]

It was upon a July evening.
At a stile I stood, looking along a path
Over the country by a second Spring
Drenched perfect green again. 'The lattermath
Will be a fine one.' So the stranger said, 5
A wandering man. Albeit I stood at rest
Flushed with desire I was. The earth outspread,
Like meadows of the future, I possessed.

And as an unaccomplished prophecy
The stranger's words, after the interval 10
Of a score years, when those fields are by me
Never to be recrossed, now I recall,
This July eve, and question, wondering,
What of the lattermath to this hoar Spring?

## 126

### *Bob's Lane*

Women he liked, did shovel-bearded Bob,
Old Farmer Hayward of the Heath, but he
Loved horses. He himself was like a cob,
And leather-coloured. Also he loved a tree.

For the life in them he loved most living things,            5
But a tree chiefly. All along the lane
He planted elms where now the stormcock sings
That travellers hear from the slow-climbing train.

Till then the track had never had a name
For all its thicket and the nightingales                     10
That should have earned it. No one was to blame.
To name a thing beloved man sometimes fails.

Many years since, Bob Hayward died, and now
None passes there because the mist and the rain
Out of the elms have turned the lane to slough               15
And gloom, the name alone survives, Bob's Lane.


## 127

### *[There was a time]*

There was a time when this poor frame was whole
And I had youth and never another care,
Or none that should have troubled a strong soul.
Yet, except sometimes in a frosty air
When my heels hammered out a melody                          5
From pavements of a city left behind,
I never would acknowledge my own glee

Because it was less mighty than my mind
Had dreamed of. Since I could not boast of strength
Great as I wished, weakness was all my boast.          10
I sought yet hated pity till at length
I earned it. Oh, too heavy was the cost.
But now that there is something I could use
My youth and strength for, I deny the age,
The care and weakness that I know—refuse          15
To admit I am unworthy of the wage
Paid to a man who gives up eyes and breath
For what can neither ask nor heed his death.


# 128

## The Green Roads

The green roads that end in the forest
Are strewn with white goose feathers this June,

Like marks left behind by some one gone to the forest
To show his track. But he has never come back.

Down each green road a cottage looks at the forest.          5
Round one the nettle towers; two are bathed in flowers.

An old man along the green road to the forest
Strays from one, from another a child alone.

In the thicket bordering the forest,
All day long a thrush twiddles his song.          10

It is old, but the trees are young in the forest,
All but one like a castle keep, in the middle deep.

That oak saw the ages pass in the forest:
They were a host, but their memories are lost,

For the tree is dead: all things forget the forest          15
Excepting perhaps me, when now I see

The old man, the child, the goose feathers at the edge of
    the forest,
And hear all day long the thrush repeat his song.


## 129

## *When first*

When first I came here I had hope,
Hope for I knew not what. Fast beat
My heart at sight of the tall slope
Of grass and yews, as if my feet

Only by scaling its steps of chalk          5
Would see something no other hill
Ever disclosed. And now I walk
Down it the last time. Never will

My heart beat so again at sight
Of any hill although as fair          10
And loftier. For infinite
The change, late unperceived, this year,

The twelfth, suddenly, shows me plain.
Hope now,—not health, nor cheerfulness,
Since they can come and go again,          15
As often one brief hour witnesses,—

Just hope has gone for ever. Perhaps
I may love other hills yet more
Than this: the future and the maps
Hide something I was waiting for.          20

One thing I know, that love with chance
And use and time and necessity
Will grow, and louder the heart's dance
At parting than at meeting be.


1 30

## The Gallows

There was a weasel lived in the sun
With all his family,
Till a keeper shot him with his gun
And hung him up on a tree,
Where he swings in the wind and rain,          5
In the sun and in the snow,
Without pleasure, without pain,
On the dead oak tree bough.

There was a crow who was no sleeper,
But a thief and a murderer                      10
Till a very late hour; and this keeper
Made him one of the things that were,
To hang and flap in rain and wind,
In the sun and in the snow.
There are no more sins to be sinned             15
On the dead oak tree bough.

There was a magpie, too,
Had a long tongue and a long tail;
He could both talk and do—
But what did that avail?                         20
He, too, flaps in the wind and rain
Alongside weasel and crow,
Without pleasure, without pain,
On the dead oak tree bough.

And many other beasts                            25
And birds, skin, bone and feather,
Have been taken from their feasts
And hung up there together,

To swing and have endless leisure
In the sun and in the snow,                                    30
Without pain, without pleasure,
On the dead oak tree bough.


## 131

## [*The Dark Forest*]

Dark is the forest and deep, and overhead
Hang stars like seeds of light
In vain, though not since they were sown was bred
Anything more bright.

And evermore mighty multitudes ride                            5
About, nor enter in;
Of the other multitudes that dwell inside
Never yet was one seen.

The forest foxglove is purple, the marguerite
Outside is gold and white,                                     10
Nor can those that pluck either blossom greet
The others, day or night.


## 132

## *When he should laugh*

When he should laugh the wise man knows full well:
For he knows what is truly laughable.
But wiser is the man who laughs also,
Or holds his laughter, when the foolish do.

## 133

## *The Swifts*

How at once should I know,
When stretched in the harvest blue
I saw the swift's black bow,
That I would not have that view
Another day                                          5
Until next May
Again it is due?

The same year after year—
But with the swift alone.
With other things I but fear                         10
That they will be over and done
Suddenly
And I only see
Them to know them gone.

## 134

## *Blenheim Oranges*

Gone, gone again,
May, June, July,
And August gone,
Again gone by,

Not memorable                                        5
Save that I saw them go,
As past the empty quays
The rivers flow.

And now again,
In the harvest rain,                                          10
The Blenheim oranges
Fall grubby from the trees,

As when I was young—
And when the lost one was here—
And when the war began                                       15
To turn young men to dung.

Look at the old house,
Outmoded, dignified,
Dark and untenanted,
With grass growing instead                                   20

Of the footsteps of life,
The friendliness, the strife;
In its beds have lain
Youth, love, age and pain:

I am something like that;                                    25
Only I am not dead,
Still breathing and interested
In the house that is not dark:—

I am something like that:
Not one pane to reflect the sun,                             30
For the schoolboys to throw at—
They have broken every one.

## 135

## [*That girl's clear eyes*] [*Sonnet* 6]

That girl's clear eyes utterly concealed all
Except that there was something to reveal.
And what did mine say in the interval?
No more: no less. They are but as a seal

Not to be broken till after I am dead;                                    5
And then vainly. Every one of us
This morning at our tasks left nothing said,
In spite of many words. We were sealed thus,
Like tombs. Nor until now could I admit
That all I cared for was the pleasure and pain           10
I tasted in the stony square sunlit,
Or the dark cloisters, or shade of airy plane,
While music blazed and children, line after line,
Marched past, hiding the 'Seventeen Thirty-Nine'.


# 136

## [*What will they do?*]

What will they do when I am gone? It is plain
That they will do without me as the rain
Can do without the flowers and the grass
That profit by it and must perish without.
I have but seen them in the loud street pass;              5
And I was naught to them. I turned about
To see them disappearing carelessly.
But what if I in them as they in me
Nourished what has great value and no price?
Almost I thought that rain thirsts for a draught         10
Which only in the blossom's chalice lies,
Until that one turned back and lightly laughed.


# 137

## The Trumpet

Rise up, rise up,
And, as the trumpet blowing
Chases the dreams of men,
As the dawn glowing

The stars that left unlit                       5
The land and water,
Rise up and scatter
The dew that covers ·
The print of last night's lovers—
Scatter it, scatter it!                          10

While you are listening
To the clear horn,
Forget, men, everything
On this earth newborn,
Except that it is lovelier                       15
Than any mysteries.
Open your eyes to the air
That has washed the eyes of the stars
Through all the dewy night:
Up with the light,                               20
To the old wars;
Arise, arise!

# 138

## [*The Child in the Orchard*]

'He rolls in the orchard: he is stained with moss
And with earth, the solitary old white horse.
Where is his father and where is his mother
Among all the brown horses? Has he a brother?
I know the swallow, the hawk, and the hern;      5
But there are two million things for me to learn.

'Who was the lady that rode the white horse
With rings and bells to Banbury Cross?
Was there no other lady in England beside
That a nursery rhyme could take for a ride?      10

The swift, the swallow, the hawk, and the hern.
There are two million things for me to learn.

'Was there a man once who straddled across
The back of the Westbury White Horse
Over there on Salisbury Plain's green wall?          15
Was he bound for Westbury, or had he a fall?
The swift, the swallow, the hawk, and the hern.
There are two million things for me to learn.

'Out of all the white horses I know three,
At the age of six; and it seems to me          20
There is so much to learn, for men,
That I dare not go to bed again.
The swift, the swallow, the hawk, and the hern.
There are millions of things for me to learn.'


139

*Lights Out*


I have come to the borders of sleep,
The unfathomable deep
Forest, where all must lose
Their way, however straight
Or winding, soon or late;          5
They can not choose.

Many a road and track
That since the dawn's first crack
Up to the forest brink
Deceived the travellers,          10
Suddenly now blurs,
And in they sink.

Here love ends—
Despair, ambition ends;

All pleasure and all trouble,                    15
Although most sweet or bitter,
Here ends, in sleep that is sweeter
Than tasks most noble.

There is not any book
Or face of dearest look                          20
That I would not turn from now
To go into the unknown
I must enter, and leave, alone,
I know not how.

The tall forest towers:                          25
Its cloudy foliage lowers
Ahead, shelf above shelf:
Its silence I hear and obey
That I may lose my way
And myself.                                      30


140

## *The long small room*

The long small room that showed willows in the west
Narrowed up to the end the fireplace filled,
Although not wide. I liked it. No one guessed
What need or accident made them so build.

Only the moon, the mouse and the sparrow peeped    5
In from the ivy round the casement thick.
Of all they saw and heard there they shall keep
The tale for the old ivy and older brick.

When I look back I am like moon, sparrow and mouse
That witnessed what they could never understand   10
Or alter or prevent in the dark house.
One thing remains the same—this my right hand

Crawling crab-like over the clean white page,
Resting awhile each morning on the pillow,
Then once more starting to crawl on towards age.                    15
The hundred last leaves stream upon the willow.


141

## *The Sheiling*

It stands alone
Up in a land of stone
All worn like ancient stairs,
A land of rocks and trees
Nourished on wind and stone.                    5

And all within
Long delicate has been;
By arts and kindliness
Coloured, sweetened, and warmed
For many years has been.                    10

Safe resting there
Men hear in the travelling air
But music, pictures see
In the same daily land
Painted by the wild air.                    15

One maker's mind
Made both, and the house is kind
To the land that gave it peace,
And the stone has taken the house
To its cold heart and is kind.                    20

## 142

### [*The Lane*]

Some day, I think, there will be people enough
In Froxfield to pick all the blackberries
Out of the hedges of Green Lane, the straight
Broad lane where now September hides herself
In bracken and blackberry, harebell and dwarf gorse.          5
Today, where yesterday a hundred sheep
Were nibbling, halcyon bells shake to the sway
Of waters that no vessel ever sailed. . . .
It is a kind of spring: the chaffinch tries
His song. For heat it is like summer too.                    10
This might be winter's quiet. While the glint
Of hollies dark in the swollen hedges lasts—
One mile—and those bells ring, little I know
Or heed if time be still the same, until
The lane ends and once more all is the same.                 15

## 143

### [*Out in the dark*]

Out in the dark over the snow
The fallow fawns invisible go
With the fallow doe;
And the winds blow
Fast as the stars are slow.                                   5

Stealthily the dark haunts round
And, when a lamp goes, without sound
At a swifter bound
Than the swiftest hound,
Arrives, and all else is drowned;                            10

And I and star and wind and deer
Are in the dark together,—near,
Yet far,—and fear
Drums on my ear
In that sage company drear.                              15

How weak and little is the light,
All the universe of sight,
Love and delight,
Before the might,
If you love it not, of night.                            20

# 1917

## 144

## *Last Poem* [*The sorrow of true love*]

The sorrow of true love is a great sorrow
And true love parting blackens a bright morrow:
Yet almost they equal joys, since their despair
Is but hope blinded by its tears, and clear
Above the storm the heavens wait to be seen.            5
But greater sorrow from less love has been
That can mistake lack of despair for hope
And knows not tempest and the perfect scope
Of summer, but a frozen drizzle perpetual
Of drops that from remorse and pity fall                10
And cannot ever shine in the sun or thaw,
Removed eternally from the sun's law.

                              13.1.17.

# NOTES

By quotations from his numerous letters, these notes are intended to provide information about Thomas's life and thinking while he was writing the poems. For many poems he seemed to draw on memories of incidents and moods that are recorded in his published prose or in his unpublished notebooks. Whenever such links can be directly established, they are included in the notes.

The following list explains the abbreviations used in the notes:

| | |
|---|---|
| *AANP* | *An Annual of New Poetry*, Constable, 1917. |
| *Berg* | Manuscript poems in the Berg Collection of the New York Public Library. |
| *Berg FNB* | Manuscript Field Note Books in the Berg Collection. |
| *BM* | Manuscript poems in the British Museum (now British Library) Add. MS. 44990. |
| *Bod* | Manuscript poems in Bodley MS. Don. d. 28. |
| *Cooke* | William Cooke, *Edward Thomas, A Critical Biography*, Faber & Faber, 1970. |
| $CP_1$ | Edward Thomas, *Collected Poems*, Selwyn & Blount, 1920. |
| $CP_2$ | Edward Thomas, *Collected Poems* (New Edition), Ingpen & Grant, 1928. |
| $CP_3$ | Edward Thomas, *Collected Poems* (New Edition), Faber & Faber, 1944. |
| $CP_4$ | Edward Thomas, *Collected Poems* (Fifth Impression), Faber & Faber, 1949. |
| *Eckert* | Robert P. Eckert, *Edward Thomas: A Biography and a Bibliography*, Dent, 1937. |
| *Eckert Coll.* | Eckert Collection: a collection of papers of Judge R. P. Eckert, now in the Bodleian Library (Eng. lett., c. 281, d. 281). |
| *EE* | 'Edward Eastaway' [Edward Thomas], *Poems*, Selwyn & Blount, 1917. |
| $EF_1$ | Manuscript poems once owned by Eleanor Farjeon. |
| $EF_2$ | Typescript poems once owned by Eleanor Farjeon. |
| *Form* | *Form, A Quarterly of the Arts*, vol. i, No. 1 (April 1916), ed. Austin O. Spare and Francis Marsden. |
| *GB* | *Letters from Edward Thomas to Gordon Bottomley*, ed. R. George Thomas, Oxford University Press, 1968. |
| *Helen* | Manuscript and typescript poems among Helen Thomas's papers. |
| *IM* | *In Memoriam: Edward Thomas, Being Number Two of the Pasture Series*, The Morland Press, July 1919. |

| | |
|---|---|
| *IPS* | Edward Thomas, *In Pursuit of Spring*, Thomas Nelson & Sons, 1914. |
| *JT* | Typescript poems once owned by the poet's brother, Julian Thomas. |
| *KS* | *Known Signatures: New Poems*, ed. John Gawsworth, Rich & Cowan, 1932 (includes *Two Poems*). |
| *LML* | Edward Thomas manuscripts in the Lockwood Memorial Library, Buffalo, New York. |
| *LP* | Edward Thomas, *Last Poems*, Selwyn & Blount, 1918. |
| $M_1$ | Manuscript poems in a green notebook once owned by the poet's son, Merfyn. |
| $M_2$ | Manuscript poems in a blue notebook once owned by the poet's son, Merfyn. |
| *MET* | Typescript poems once owned by the poet's mother, Mary Elizabeth Thomas. |
| *Moore* | John Moore, *The Life and Letters of Edward Thomas*, Heinemann, 1939. |
| *NS* | 'Edward Eastaway' [Edward Thomas], *Four Poems*, in *New Statesman*, 28 April 1917, p. 87. |
| *Poetry* | *Poetry: A Magazine of Verse*, ed. Harriet Monroe, vol. ix, No. V, February 1917, pp. 247–50 [Poems by Edward Eastaway], Chicago. |
| *RB* | *Root and Branch, A Seasonal of the Arts*, ed. James Guthrie 1913–18 (vol. i: 1913–15; vol. ii: 1916–18). |
| $RF_1$ | Poems included in letters from Thomas to Robert Frost, in Dartmouth College Library, Hanover, New Hampshire, U.S.A. |
| $RF_2$ | Typescript poems among the Robert Frost papers in Dartmouth College Library. |
| $RGT_1$ | Manuscript poem given to the editor by Helen Thomas. |
| $RGT_2$ | Typescript poems given to the editor by Helen Thomas. |
| *RLW* | Manuscript poems given by Eleanor Farjeon to the late Rowland L. Watson (Secretary to the Edward Thomas Memorial Fund). |
| *SP* | 'Edward Eastaway' [Edward Thomas], *Six Poems*, The Pear Tree Press, Flansham, Sussex, 1916. |
| *TE* | *This England, An Anthology from her Writers*, compiled by Edward Thomas, Oxford University Press, 1915. |
| *TLFY* | Eleanor Farjeon, *Edward Thomas: The Last Four Years*, Oxford University Press, 1958. |
| *TP* | *Twelve Poets, A Miscellany of New Verse*, Selwyn & Blount, 1918. |
| *Two Poems* | Edward Thomas, *Two Poems*, Ingpen & Grant, 1927. |

———

## 1 *Up in the Wind*

35 The White Horse is an inn at Froxfield, near Steep.

The following jottings are in *Berg FNB* 79.

27 November 1914. *Ryton*: Clothes on the line violently blowing in wind and crackle like a rising woodfire. [Cf. ll. 95-6.]

On the left-hand side, facing an entry dated 2 Nov. 1914:

> I could wring the old girl's neck
> That put it here
> A public house! (Charcoal burner)
> by bringing up and quite outdoing
> The idea of London
> Two woods around and never a road in sight
> Trees roaring like a train without an end
> But she's dead long ago
> Only a motorist from far away
> Or marketers in carts once a fortnight
> Or a few fresh tramps ignorant
> of the house turning.

The next page (undated) is headed:

### Subjects

(1) The White Horse
(2) Old Man (see this notebook for Nov. 11)
(1) dirty earth and clean bright sky.

> see 1 December back. [i.e. back of the notebook]

## 2 *November Sky*

See the following jottings from *Berg FNB* 79:

1 December 1914. The roads all muddy with mashed leaves, twigs, sparse hedges, and sodden fields—

Beautiful hobnail pattern in path over reddish light ploughland

Undated, but transferred to 1 Dec. 1914:

A fine liquid morning then sunny drops slanting a *few* in a sprinkle then heavy rain and a blue and black sky where wind comes from. Then at 12-3 bright sun, clear sweet cold sky with a few white clouds line—the sky so bright and clear and cleaner. The roads all muddy with mashed leaves and twigs, and bare hedges and sodden fields. Clear till moon rise (big full white moon towards East and sun going crimson cloudless in West—When Jupiter was visible at 4.45 there was some wet sandcoloured cloud in West—a big rag of it.—Beautiful hobnail pattern on path near reddish bright ploughland. An evening of alternate blazing moon and wind and of lashing rain. Each long stick in faggots has been dipped in moonlight once: also water spouts. gutters.

## 3 *March*

In this poem Thomas takes seriously Frost's advice that he should write verse based on his prose book *In Pursuit of Spring* (1914). The first three lines reflect the structure of that travel book which is hung around the thin thread of a search for the true spring after so many false starts. See *IPS*, pp. 24-5 ('In search of Spring') and pp. 290-301 ('The Grave of Winter'). This poem is dated in *LML* with a heavy relief pen which is used for all the final corrections made to 'Up in the Wind' and 'November Sky' and which suggests that by 5 Dec. 1914 Thomas had decided to commit himself firmly both to writing verse and to following Frost's advice.

## 4 *Old Man*

The poem owes a great deal to Thomas's spate of autobiographical writing in the autumn and winter of 1912 (see *GB*, Letter 126), of which *The Childhood of Edward Thomas* (published in 1937 but probably written 1912-13) is a part. Its opening paragraphs are relevant to 'Old Man':

> When I penetrate backward into my childhood I come perhaps sooner than many people to impassable night. A sweet darkness enfolds with a faint blessing my life up to the age of about four. . . . But out of doors, somewhere at the verge of the dark years, I can recall more vividly and completely than any spent indoors at that time one day above others. I lay in the tall grass and buttercups of a narrow field at the edge of London and saw the sky and nothing but the sky. There was some one near, probably a servant, necessary but utterly insignificant. I was alone and happy to be so, just as indoors I was happy among people and shadows between walls. Was it one day or many? I know of no beginning or end to it; but an end I suppose it had an age past. [pp. 13-14]

See, (1) in *Berg holograph notebook* No. 3, dated on the flyleaf by Thomas, 10 Aug. 1909, the following extract from an unpublished story called *The Old House*:

> Mrs Rose [a housekeeper] was stirring in the garden. She appeared among the trees. 'Do you know what this is, Sir?' she asked as he [Mr. Banks, the owner of the house] got up. It was a feathery sprig of grey green. Without thinking he crushed it gently between his fingers and held it to his nose. 'Ah!—Beautiful.' [Beginning of an insertion from the left-hand side.] He sniffed a long and solemn exploring sniff, to the heart of the scent, and then again; and then he meditated with the sprig at his nose but no longer smelling it; and then he tried to think and smell at the same time, closing his eyes, as if he were diving through some new medium into a strange land,—but in vain.' [End of insertion.] 'No, what is it?' 'Lad's love, sir. Crush it and it is sweeter.'

> Again 'Blenheim 1705' [a date on a lintel of the Old House] ran in his brain he knew not why. The scent was like memory.

(2) *Berg FNB* 79, entry dated 11 Nov. 1914:

> '*Old Man* scent, I smell again and again not really liking it but venerating it because it holds the secret of something of very long ago which I feel it may someday recall, but I have got no idea what.'

## 5  *The Signpost*

A rough outline of this poem is in *Berg FNB* 79, not later than December 1914. The right-hand side of page 5 from the end of the notebook has the single line

A        to<br>
The mouthful of earth that remedies all.

The left-hand side reads:

When the grass is heard first<br>
And the crimson haunts the boughs<br>
With smoke of traveller's joy<br>
Today I wished I was (fifty) 20

When I - - -<br>
  - - - - -<br>
Then I wished I had not been born<br>
——————

When -<br>
And I ~~am~~ 50, what shall I wish<br>
——————

When -<br>
Will there come a day<br>
When I could wish to be alive<br>
Somehow 20 or 40 or not

## 6  *The Other*

This poem had a special interest for Frost, who had directed Thomas's attention specifically to *IPS* as evidence of Thomas's poetic ability. 'The Other' is closely based on 'The Other Man' in *IPS*, and both poets shared an interest in the hallucinatory recurrence it describes.

Passages on the following pages in *IPS* demonstrate the prose genesis of the poem: pp. 43-4, 47-9, 51-2, 60, 119-27, 140, 201-15, 218-32, and 282.

*53-4* Cf. the conversations between Thomas and the 'other man' in *IPS* (pp. 119-27), especially his 'confession' about his fondness for clay pipes; see also pp. 219-20, where the 'other man' speaks of the poet and his life-long habit of using field notebooks:

> He rambled on and on about himself, his past, his writing, his digestion; his main point being that he did not like writing. He had been attempting the impossible task of reducing undigested notes about all sorts of details to a grammatical, continuous narrative. He abused notebooks violently. He said that they blinded him to nearly everything that would not go into the form of notes; or, at any rate, he could never afterwards reproduce the great effects of Nature and fill in the interstices merely—which was all they were good for—from the notes. The notes—often of things which he would otherwise have forgotten—had to fill the whole canvas. Whereas, if he had taken none, then only the important, what

he truly cared for, would have survived in his memory, arranged not perhaps as they were in Nature, but at least according to the tendencies of his own spirit. 'Good God!' said he. But luckily we were by this time on the level. I mounted. He followed.

*61-70* Cf. Thomas's 'pleasure of my disembodied spirit (so to call it)' on the cycle ride from Semington and Melksham to Staverton (*IPS*, pp. 201-15). The passage concludes:

The inn door, which was now open, was as the entrance to a bright cave in the middle of the darkness: the illumination had a kind of blessedness such as it might have had to a cow, not without foreignness; and a half-seen man within it belonged to a world, blessed indeed, but far different from this one of mine, dark, soft, and tranquil. I felt that I could walk on thus, sipping the evening silence and solitude, endlessly. But at the house where I was staying I stopped as usual. I entered, blinked at the light, and by laughing at something, said with the intention of being laughed at, I swiftly again naturalized myself.

*80* Cf. *IPS*, p. 60, where Thomas writes of George Meredith: 'From first to last he wrote as an inhabitant of this earth, where, as Wordsworth says, "we have our happiness or not at all," just or unjust.'

Two entries in the *Berg FNB* bear on this poem.

(1) *Berg FNB* 62, June 1913, reads: '*Other Man*—wraith—when seen at Salterley I was not sure he had existed before—he avoids a difficulty in telling truth.'

(2) *Berg FNB* 67, 18 Dec. 1913, reads:

*East Grinstead.* 4.30. One of those eternal evenings—the wind gone, no one upon the road. I grasp the stately tall holly or look over the ploughland to the near ridge, the crocketed spruces, the dark house mass, and behind them a soft dulling flame-coloured sky where large shapeless soft dull dark clouds in roughly horizontal lines are massing with one bright star in an interstice—and far behind me an owl calls again and again and somewhere far to one side in a hid hollow a dog barks and nearer, one or two blackbirds climb as they fly along hedges. What does it mean? I feel an old inhabitant of earth at such times. How many hundred times have I seen the same since I was fifteen.

## 10 *The Mountain Chapel*

The poem appears to be based on memories of early visits to Wales. Cf. Thomas's *Beautiful Wales* (1905), p. 26 and pp. 148-9:

But Siloh stands firm, and ventures once a week to send up a thin music that avails nothing against the wind; although close to it, threatening it, laughing at it, able to overwhelm it, should the laugh become cruel, is a company of elder trees, which, seen at twilight, are sentinels, embossed upon the sky—sentinels of the invisible, patient, unconquerable powers: or (if one is lighter-hearted) they seem the empty homes of what the mines and the chapels think they have routed . . .

But by this mountain you cannot be really at ease until in some way you have travelled through all history. For it has not been as nothing to it that Persia, Carthage, Greece and Rome, and Spain have been great and are not. It has been worn by the foot-prints of time which have elsewhere made the grass a little deeper or renewed the woods. It has sat motionless, looking on the world; it has grown wrinkled; it is all memory. Were it and its fellows to depart, we should not know how old we were; for we should have only books. Therefore I love it. It offers no illusions. Its roads are winding and rough. The grass is thin; the shelter scarce, the valley crops moderate; the cheese and mutton good; the water pure; the people strong, kind, intelligent, and without newspapers; the fires warm and bright and large, and throwing light and shadow upon pewter and brass and oak and books. It offers no illusions; for it is clear, as it is not in a city or in an exuberant English county, that the world is old and troubled, and that light and warmth and fellowship are good. Sometimes comes a thought that it is a huge gravestone, so it is worn, so obscure and brief its legend. It belongs to the past, to the dead; and the dead, as they are more numerous, so here they are greater than we, and we only great because we shall one day be of their number. You cannot look at it without thinking that the time will come when it may be, and we are not, nor the races of men—

> *sed haec prius fuere: nunc recondita*
> *senet quiete.*

## 11 *The Manor Farm*

*This England, An Anthology from her Writers*, compiled by Thomas (1915) is described by him in a prefatory note:

> This is an anthology from the work of English writers rather strictly so called. Building round a few most English poems like 'When icicles hang by the wall',—excluding professedly patriotic writing because it is generally bad and because indirect praise is sweeter and more profound,—never aiming at what a committee from Great Britain and Ireland might call complete,—I wished to make a book as full of English character and country as an egg is of meat. If I have reminded others, as I did myself continually, of some of the echoes called up by the name of England, I am satisfied.

Apart from some prose quotations from C. M. Doughty and W. H. Hudson, and a few songs from three volumes of folk-songs, the only contemporary poems in the selection are by Gordon Bottomley, Walter de la Mare, Thomas Hardy, and Edward Eastaway ('Haymaking' and 'The Manor Farm' in Section III, 'Her Sweet Three Corners', pp. 111-12).

## 12 *An Old Song* [1]

4 *BM*'s cancelled 'O' (in favour of 'But') gave the original refrain of the Lincolnshire folk-song, 'The Lincolnshire Poacher', whose words and music are included in Thomas's *The Pocket Book of Poems and Songs for the Open Air* (p. 81) which, together with his letters to Gordon Bottomley, give some indication of his informed interest in ballads and folk-music.

*13* The incident with a gamekeeper occurred on a visit to Robert Frost at The Gallows, near Dymock. Apparently Frost resented the threats of Lord Beauchamp's shot-gun-carrying gamekeeper and gave him a piece of his mind. Thomas was frightened, but Frost, in a typical rage, went back and threatened to beat up the man. The police later intervened and finally Lord Beauchamp sent Frost an apology. References to this incident occur frequently in Thomas's letters to Frost. The affair and its background is described in Lawrance Thompson, *Robert Frost: The Early Years* (London, 1967), pp. 467-8.

## 13 *An Old Song* [2]

*19-22* Cf. this excerpt from Thomas's letter to his brother-in-law, Hugh McArthur, from Steep, dated 26 Mar. 1912: 'We've had a very good time for us. I kept it up till 1 o'clock this morning with sea songs by a new neighbour—a man who was on the "Nimrod" with Shackleton . . .'

## 14 *The Combe*

Roman figure II is inserted before the title in *JT* and the poem is signed 'Edward Eastaway', the only known autograph of this pseudonym. Presumably the poem was among the first group of verses sent to editors (e.g. Monro and Blackwood's) and rejected in December 1914 and January 1915.

## 15 *The Hollow Wood*

'The Hollow Land' is a poem by William Morris, whose *Collected Works* Thomas had reviewed between September and December 1914. The name was also given to a copse near Gordon Bottomley's home at Carnforth.

## 16 *The New Year*

*7-8* This image is taken from the prose version of 'Up in the Wind' in *LML* (see Appendix A, p. 435).

*1-12* These games are described in *The Childhood of Edward Thomas*, pp. 79-80:

> The playground was asphalt; again there were no organized games, but a dozen groups playing leap frog, fly the garter, or tops, or chasing one another, or simply messing about.

'Fly the garter'—if that is its right name—was a grand game to see played by a dozen of the biggest boys. I forget how it came about, but by degrees at length there were four or five boys bent double, forming a continuous line of backs. Each grasped the one in front of him and the first of them had his head, protected by his hands, against the playground wall. From half-way across the playground a big boy ran at a gallop, his ironshod heels pounding the asphalt, towards this line of boys who could see him approaching between their legs. Reaching the line and putting his hands upon the first back to help him leap he leaped forward into the air. A brilliant leaper would use only one hand for the take off: the other gave a sonorous smack on the right place in passing. With legs outspread he flew along the line of backs, and alighted upon the fourth or fifth of them. The lighter his weight, the more fortunate was the steed thus accidentally mounted: the heavier, the greater was the chance that both together crashed to the ground. Then, I think, the leaper added another to the line of backs and set the next leaper an impossible task.

(This game was common in the editor's own primary school in the Rhymney Valley between 1920 and 1924. It was called 'Cutter'—an anglicized form of Welsh 'cwtaf', i.e. 'the tailender'; probably a Middle Welsh borrowing from Middle English 'cut', i.e. 'a lot'.)

## 20 *Snow*

3 The child in the poem is the poet's younger daughter, Myfanwy. The best source of incidental background information to these early poems is *TLFY*, pp. 107-55. For Thomas's interest in tales written for children see especially his *Celtic Stories* (1911), *Norse Tales* (1912), and *Four-and-Twenty Blackbirds* (1915), and, variously, his numerous favourable reviews of Walter de la Mare's prose and poetry.

## 21 *Adlestrop*

Adlestrop is on the main road between Stow-on-the-Wold and Chipping Norton (about five miles from Stow-on-the-Wold). The station, now closed, was close to the River Evenlode and half a mile away from the village. It was on the main G.W.R. line from Oxford to Worcester and Wolverhampton, and in Thomas's day was part of the Central Line.

An undated entry (probably early January 1915) in *Berg FNB* 80 reads: 'Train stopping outside station at Adlestrop June 1914.' This incident is expanded in *Berg FNB* 75:

23 June 1914. A glorious day from 4.20 a.m. and at 10 tiers above tiers of white cloud with dirtiest grey bars above the sea of slate and dull brick by Battersea Park. Then at Oxford tiers of pure white with loose longer masses above and gaps of dark clear blue above hay-making and elms.

Then we stopped at Adlestrop, through the willows could be heard a chain of blackbirds' songs at 12.45 and one thrush and no man seen, only a hiss of engine letting off steam.

Stopping outside Campden by banks of long grass, willowherb and meadowsweet, extraordinary silence between two periods of travel—looking out on grey dry stones between metals and the shining metals and over it all the elms willows and long grass—one man clears his throat—a greater than rustic silence. No house in view. Stop only for a minute till signal is up.

Now stop like this outside Colwall on 27th with thrush singing on hillside above road.

24-27th. At Ledington with Frost in always hot weather.

## 24 *The Lofty Sky*

This poem was written, after seven days in bed with an injured ankle, on Thomas's first day 'downstairs but worse off because I know how helpless I still am. I can only hop and am in a filthy temper.' (Letter in *TLFY*, 10 Jan. 1915.)

## 25 *The Cuckoo*

For a different memory see Thomas's essay, 'The First Cuckoo' in *The Last Sheaf* (1928), pp. 60-4.

## 26 *Swedes*

Cf. Thomas's *The Heart of England* (1906), Ch. I, p. 19:

Or as, when a man has mined in the dead desert for many days, he suddenly enters an old tomb, and making a light, sees before him vases of alabaster, furniture adorned with gold and blue enamel and the figures of gods, a chariot of gold, and a silence perfected through many ages in the company of death and of the desire of immortality.

*11 Amen-hotep* was the name used in Thomas's day for the Egyptian ruler Armen-ophis II (1436-1413 B.C.). The tomb-robber in the poem may refer to an incident in the Valley of Kings' tombs in November 1901 (see J. H. Breasted, *A History of the Ancient Egyptians* (1912)).

## 27 *The Unknown Bird*

*15-19* Although Thomas had edited *The Book of the Open Air* (1907) and written much on country topics, he did not consider himself a professional naturalist like his friend W. H. Hudson whose *Adventures among Birds* is praised in *IPS*, pp. 244-50: 'While his birds are intensely alive in many different ways, and always intensely birdlike, presenting a loveliness beyond that of idealized or super-naturalized women and children, yet at the same time their humanity was never before so apparent.'

See *Berg FNB* early in January 1915 for a single line: 'The strange bird la!—la!—la!'

## 29 [*Man and Dog*]

For Thomas's interest in the authentic life of tramps, blended with some auto-biographical overtones, see the following quotation from 'Hawthornden', *Light and Twilight* (1911), pp. 123-6:

> When he moved into the country he was prepared for adventures. Gypsies should be allowed to camp near his house and he would be familiar with them. He would invite the tramps into his study for a talk and a smoke. He used to sit by the roadside, or in the tap-room of an inn, waiting for what would turn up. But something always stood in the way—himself. He grew tired of paying for a tramp's quart, and was disconcerted, now by too great familiarity and now by too great respect. When a tramp came to the back door, his maids or his wife reported it to him, and they sometimes had interesting fragments of a story to relate; for the women had human sympathies along with unquestioning common-place views of social distinctions. Sometimes he saw the man coming or going, and formed romantic conjectures which made him impatient of what he actually heard.

See a detailed prose account of this meeting in *Berg FNB* 79, dated 21 Nov. 1914:

> Going up Stoner in cold strong N.E. wind but a fine cloudy sky at 3, overtook short stiff oldish man taking short quick strides—carrying flag basket and brolly and old coat on back and with a green ash stick in hand. Says it's a fine day and as I passed he decides to ask me for—I don't know. I stopped his request with questions, found him a 6d. He had a little bitch brown with spots of grey reminding me of a Welsh sheep-dog—not much one, but company. He says the mother was almost pure (blue) Welsh. Hunts in Hangers, nearly got one this morning 'he would and he wouldn't, 'twas like that.' 'They say those Welsh bitches will breed with a fox. He knew one the other side of Guildford and she had her litter of seven in a rabbit-hole. He had one. It tried to bite anything it killed so hard it was useless: red mouth like a fox.' He had come from Childgrove where he's done two halfdays dock-picking this week: is going to Alton and hopes for a lift from Crowley's men to Longmoor to look for a job. But perhaps he won't reach Alton—rheumatism in one leg—rubs oil they sell at harness makers and 'supples' it a bit—round face with white bristles all over and eyes with red rims. Has worked a lot at S'hampton docks, navvying, but likes farm work best, has promises of flint picking when the sheep are out of field, but can't hang about—comes from Christchurch in the New Forest—did a year's soldiering in '74 with Berkshires—has three sons at Front, one just come from Bombay had really finished his eight years with the colours, one son a marine. If he can't reach Alton, will get a shakedown from a farmer.
>
> Talked about the soldiers just coming to billet in Petersfield—he thought two or three thousand—twenty, or so, in kilts—might be a Border Regiment.
>
> A rustic, burring, rather monotonous speech, head a little hung down, but hardly a stoop as he keeps on at his stiff quick short steps among crisp dry scurrying leaves up to Ludcombe Corner where I turned off.
>
> He was thinking about soldiers in France—terrible affair—in cold weather, supposing they would be 'marching after the enemy' and surely not lying in trenches this winter weather.

## 30 *Beauty*

See Thomas's letter to James Guthrie, dated 21 Mar. 1915 [1916?]:

> The book [*Six Poems*] arrived yesterday. . . . There are two words omitted that should be
> inserted by hand. In the last line [*sic*] of 'Beauty' 'my' should be inserted before 'rest'
> 'There I find my rest'. In 'Aspens' [Poem 83], last verse, the line should be 'We cannot
> other than an aspen be'. insert 'an'. That can be managed, can't it?

## 31 [*The Gypsy*]

Thomas's fascination with gipsy life can be seen in the 'Conclusion' to his *George
Borrow: The Man and His Books* (1912). See especially pp. 319–20:

> Wistful or fancifully envious admiration for the fortunate simple yeomen, or careless
> poor men, or noble savages, or untradesmanlike fishermen, or unromanized *Germani*, or
> animals who do not fret about their souls, admiration for those in any class who are not
> for the fashion of these days, is a deep-seated and ancient sentiment, akin to the sentiment
> for childhood and the golden age. Borrow met a hundred men fit to awaken and satisfy
> this admiration in an age when thousands can over-eat and over-dress in comfort all the
> days of their life. Sometimes he shows that he himself admires in this way, but more often
> he mingles with them as one almost on an equality with them, though his melancholy or
> his book knowledge is at times something of a foil. He introduces us to fighting men,
> jockeys, thieves, and rat-catchers, without our running any risk of contamination. Above
> all, he introduces us to the Gypsies, people who are either young and beautiful or strong,
> or else witchlike in a fierce old age. . . .
> Borrow's Gypsies are wild and uncoddled and without sordidness, and will not soon
> be superseded. They are painted with a lively if ideal colouring, and they live only in his
> books. They will not be seen again until the day of Jefferies' wild England, 'after London,'
> shall come, and tents are pitched amidst the ruins of palaces that had displaced earlier
> tents. Borrow's England is the old England of Fielding, painted with more intensity
> because even as Borrow was travelling the change was far advanced, and when he was
> writing had been fulfilled. And now most people have to keep off the grass, except in
> remotest parts or in the neighbourhood of large towns where landowners are, to some
> extent, kept in their place. The rivers, the very roads, are not ours, as they were Borrow's.
> We go out to look for them still, and of those who adventure with caravan, tent, or knap-
> sack, the majority must be consciously under Borrow's influence.

See *Berg FNB* 67 for the incidents behind this poem:

*East Grinstead*. 11th December 1913. *East Grinstead Fair*

Drawn up at fork to Turner's Hill etc. are a lot of little traps and small rough ponies.
A balloon seller.

Gypsies coming in with sham flowers and 'My lucky gentleman' 'You've got a lucky face'.
But she had a much luckier face in reality. Lots of caravans drawn up between Selsfield
and Grinstead—begging money or half pipe of tobacco. One caravan on Selsfield Common,
several down by Tickeridge, others by Hill Farm, more at fork to Saint Hill. All begging.
One boy and girl I ran away from. One boy playing rapid rascally Bacchanal tune on mouth
organ while he drums on a tambourine and stamps feet and workmen grin. A few cart-
horses at auction. Cheapjack, little blackhaired pale man of 30 who asks a rough and

simple labourer if he's married and says 'You have my sympathy' and shakes hands and says 'Do you love your wife?' Lots of laughing, knives, clocks, jewellry [*sic*] etc.

*17 December.* Two more gypsies with that rascally Bacchic music at Selsfield House door, one has mouth organ, the other drums on tambourine, lacking cymbals—they play 'Over the hills and far away' and 'If I were Mr. Balfour'.

*4.15 p.m.* How different two days ago when I looked from a highish road (? or from railway near Warnham) over a houseless lowish but hollow wooded country, nothing but gradations of inhuman dark (beginning to get misty at nightfall), as of an underworld and my soul fled over it experiencing the afterdeath—friendless, vacant hopeless.

## 32 [*Ambition*]

*18-23* The mood reflected in these lines resembles the following passage from *IPS*, pp. 210-11:

Motion was extraordinarily easy that afternoon, and I had no doubts that I did well to bicycle instead of walking. It was as easy as riding in a cart, and more satisfying to a restless man. At the same time I was a great deal nearer to being a disembodied spirit than I can often be. I was not at all tired, so far as I knew. No people or thoughts embarrassed me. I fed through the senses directly, but very temperately, through the eyes chiefly, and was happier than is explicable or seems reasonable. This pleasure of my disembodied spirit (so to call it) was an inhuman and diffused one, such as may be attained by whatever dregs of this our life survive after death. In fact, had I to describe the adventure of this remnant of a man I should express it somewhat thus, with no need of help from Dante, Mr. A. C. Benson, or any other visitors to the afterworld. In a different mood I might have been encouraged to believe the experience a foretaste of a sort of imprisonment in the viewless winds, or of a spiritual share in the task of keeping the cloudy winds 'fresh for the opening of the morning's eye.' Supposing I were persuaded to provide this afterworld with some of the usual furniture, I could borrow several visible things from that ride through Semington, Melksham, and Staverton.

(Cf. notes to 'The Other', Poem 6.)

## 34 *Parting*

*13* The poet's son, Merfyn, left Steep with his mother for Liverpool on 11 Feb. and embarked for America two days later with Robert Frost and his family. (Thomas was unable to walk because of an ankle injury.) The poem recalls the complicated relationship between father and son which is best expressed in Thomas's letters to Bottomley (*GB*, especially Letters 146, 162, and 163).

*24* 'like this' refers to the poem. 'stir or stain' may refer to the actual manuscript (as well as the act of memory); the page in *BM* is blotted in a few places.

## 36  *May 23*

The day after writing this poem Thomas left Steep for the first time since an ankle injury had confined him there since early January. He spent a few days checking source material for his anthology *This England* and returned to Steep on 29 Feb. 1915.

*30-5* For Jack's reluctance to sell his ware, compare the Watercress Man in *The Heart of England* (1906), Ch. I ('Leaving Town'), which suggests that Jack Noman was a composite character based on memories that began with Thomas's youthful encounter with some such wanderer when he was a boy of nine.

## 38  *Home* [1]

*14, 16* The words 'there' and 'here', I suggest, refer directly to Thomas's parents' home at Balham—he had spent two days with them the previous week and discovered that his mother needed an operation for cataract—and his own home at Steep.

*17-20* An oblique reference to Thomas's many disagreements with his father. (See also note on Poem 99.)

## 39  *The Owl*

See *An Introduction* by Edward Garnett to *Selected Poems* (The Gregynog Press, 1927), p. vi: 'Three months before his death, Thomas was still insistent that "Edward Eastaway's" real name should not be disclosed to editors. I took "Home" and "The Owl" (re-entitled "Those Others") to *The Nation* in January 1917.'
  See *Berg FNB* 77: '*20 October 1914*. (After returning from Swansea and Ryton). Day ends silent and misty: owl hoots, blackbirds chink, a robin sings, far off train roars hollowly in the Vale [of Steep].'

## 40  *The Child on the Cliff*

The child was probably Edward's brother Julian. See letter to Eleanor Farjeon (*TLFY*, pp. 127-8), dated 25 Mar. 1915: 'I like the Child on the Cliff. It is a memory between one of my young brothers and myself which he reminded me of lately. [A note in Julian's diary on 24 Feb. stated that 'Edwy was at Balham last week'.] He was most of the child and I have been truthful. I think I can expect some allowances for the "strangeness" of the day.' The poet's childhood summer holidays were spent with relations in West Wales and I suggest that the cliffs in the poem refer either to Gower or Laugharne, both places that Thomas visited frequently throughout his life.

## 41 *The Bridge*

The reflective mood of this poem probably refers to the first letter received from Frost and Merfyn after they landed in New York. See letter to Eleanor Farjeon (*TLFY*, p. 124) dated 12 Mar. 1915: 'But I am sick of reading at the Museum and then Maeterlinck's poems. I was glad to get back here and go up to the study again and write and have fine days for sowing the garden. I am not sure that I want to leave this part after all [to join Frost in the U.S.A.], especially as it would cost so much.' The 'strange bridge' (l. 2) may well refer to his first half-unconscious decision to enlist and to exorcise the indecision that had marked his life for nearly three years.

## 44 *The New House*

This is the house at Wick Green which was built for Thomas by Geoffrey Lupton in 1909. See 'Wind and Mist' (Poem 54) and *GB* (especially Letters 104, 105, 107, 126).

## 45 *The Barn and the Down*

See *Berg FNB* 80, undated, before 25 Mar. 1915: 'At end of Charles Street is a big slate-barn. You see the length of it and its ridge is in evening like Down against sky and sometimes I mistake a Down (which is also visible from thereabouts) for the barn—sometimes barn is exalted, sometimes Down humbled.'

## 46 *Sowing*

The *BM* manuscript has a fifth stanza:

> A kiss for all the seeds'
> Dry multitude,
> A tear at ending this
> March interlude.

This final rejected stanza, with its 'calendar-verse' tone, echoes Thomas's sense of happiness before he began work on another 'filthy job—a book on the Duke of Marlborough to be done in haste'. See *TLFY*, pp. 127-8 and especially a letter to Eleanor Farjeon of 25 Mar. 1915: 'The weather has been tempting and tiring. We have done a lot of gardening, and never had the ground in better order so early.'

## 47 *March the 3rd*

3 Mar. was the poet's birthday.

## 48 *Two Pewits*

See Thomas's letter to Edward Garnett (in *Selected Poems* (The Gregynog Press, 1927), p. xi, written in March–April 1915):

> But I can't tell you how pleased I am that you like the long piece [Lob] in the main and 'Pewits' too. I am going to try and be just about the lines you have marked in 'Pewits', though I am not sure whether you question the form of them or the 'divagations' of the idea, but probably the latter. If only I could hit upon some continuous form as you suggest. I doubt if it will come by direct consideration. But I think perhaps intermingled prose and verse would add a difficulty. Even as it is I fancy the better passages in my prose lose by not really being happy in their place.

(Garnett probably marked ll. 12–15.)

## 50 *The Path*

The path was probably the short cut taken by Thomas each morning as he walked from his home in Steep village to his study up on Wick Green adjacent to the new house Lupton had built for him. See his letter to Eleanor Farjeon (*TLFY*, p. 127), dated 25 Mar. 1915, about some more poems he had written: 'It has perhaps become a really bad habit as I walk up the hill and I can sometimes hardly wait to light my fire.'

## 51 [*The Wasp Trap*]

See *Berg FNB* 80: '*25 March 1915*: Beautiful moonlight and in hedge glistens bottle put there long ago for wasps—old time—old crockery opposite cottages—far [lakes] ponds etc.'

## 52 *A Tale* [Cancelled version]

See *Berg FNB* 80: '*25 March 1915* [cont.]. Outside the [old] ruined cottage is periwinkle and when that is not flowering there is some blue and white peering among the leaves.'

## 54 *Wind and Mist*

*1* The 'view' is the one seen across the South Downs from near the poet's study where the poem was written, close to the new house at Wick Green where he lived from 1909 to 1913. The encounter imagined in the poem would have taken place near Berryfield Cottage (where Thomas had lived before the building of this new house).

*44-7* For the garden see *GB*, especially Letters 104, 107, 108; and 115 (dated 23 Feb. 1911): 'The garden improves but the clay breaks first the back and then the heart.'

*46-7* See *Berg FNB* 80, undated, before 25 Mar. 1915:

> First I broke my back and then my heart
> But the back will not mend.

*54* For the significance of the phrase 'cloud castle' in Thomas's earlier private symbolism see his short sketch 'Cloud Castle', written in 1912 and printed posthumously in *Cloud Castle and Other Papers* (1922).


## 56 *Lob*

Thomas's life-long interest in folk-tales, and place-names, and country lore of all kinds is copiously illustrated in his *Richard Jefferies* (1909), *Celtic Stories* (1911), *The Country* (1913), *The Icknield Way* (1913), *Four-and-Twenty Blackbirds* (1915), and *This England* (1915). His most general statement of this interest is best shown in the following quotation from his introduction to Isaac Taylor, *Words and Places* (No. 517 of *Everyman's Library*), 1911:

> Remembering the 'too ingenious antiquary' and the fearless folk etymology which created the 'liver' for Liverpool, Mr. [J. H.] Round disputes the philologist's claim to explain place names by his laws, because . . . 'they ignore the human element.' But they ignore only what is incalculable, and when they confess defeat they are bowing partly to darkest antiquity and partly to this very human element. . . . I found a sturdy fellow sitting on Offa's Dyke in Monmouthshire who told me that the mound was 'Dogger's Bank.' We have need of men like that to explain 'Eggpie' Lane near the village of Sevenoaks Weald, or Tumbling Bay in a neighbouring parish far inland. . . . Science goes deep, but the pure sense goes deeper.' A useful guide to the many folk-tales in *Lob* is *English Fairy Tales*, ed. J. Jacobs (1890-94).

*Lob*: a name variously used for a country bumpkin, a kind of a clown, or mischievous Puck-like fairy (especially in this last in the form *Lob-lie-by-the-fire*). See, too, the poem 'Lob Lie by the Fire' in De la Mare's *A Child's Day* (1912).

*26 Weathercock*: see note to l. 123 (*Gotham*).

*65-6 Gerard*. Thomas quotes John Gerard's *The Herball* (1597) on 'Traveller's Joy' in *TE*, p. 97.

*73-4* See *Berg FNB* 80, undated, between 25 Mar. and 18 Apr. 1915:

> 'Twas she first called the Hog's back the Hog's Back
> And gave the name to Mother Dunch's Buttocks.

*74 Mother Dunch's Buttocks*, according to Camden's *Brittania* a vulgar name for Sinodun Hill, Berkshire, gave offence to one editor to whom he offered 'Lob' soon after it was written.

*96 tall Tom*: see *Love's Labour's Lost*, v. ii. 909-27, quoted in *TE*, p. 51.

*99 Herne the Hunter*: a ghostly medieval hunter, originally a keeper in Windsor Forest, who is described by Mistress Page in *The Merry Wives of Windsor*, IV. iv. 28-40. Quoted under the title *Herne the Hunter* in *TE*, p. 72.

*104-12, 122-9* For the various tales of 'Jack', including 'The Princess of Canterbury', see Jacobs, *English Fairy Tales*.

*123 Gotham's sages*. From medieval times, at least, the people of Gotham in Nottinghamshire acquired a reputation for foolish behaviour. Many tales, some involving weathercocks or hedging in a cuckoo or finding the moon in a pond, had accumulated around the Wise Men of Gotham. The first known collection, 'Merry Tales of Gotham by A.B.' is extant in a 1630 edition.

*113-22* This tale, from Charlotte S. Burne, *Shropshire Folk-Lore*, is quoted in *TE*, pp. 68-9.

*137 Robin Hood*. Thomas quotes one of the many Robin Hood ballads in *TE*, pp. 22-4. Apart from the names of flowers, folk-tales of 'Robin' can be found in Jacobs (above).

61 *Home* [2]

This poem seems to confirm the subtle relationship between Thomas's sudden development as a poet and his way of life at Steep. It was composed after his first longish working period spent away from home since he had begun to write verse in late November and early December 1914. (From 5 Apr. 1915 he had spent a few days with his parents at Balham in order to work at the British Museum on his newly commissioned life of the Duke of Marlborough.)

    See *Berg FNB* 80, 12 Apr. 1915: 'Evening of misty stillness after drizzly day—last thrushes on oaks—then man goes by a dark white cottage front to thatched wood lodge and presently began sawing and birds were all still.'

62 [*Health*]

See *Berg FNB* 80, undated, after 18 Apr. and before 23 May 1915: 'The best and worst of sickness is to think how glorious health is or might be.—glorious ambitious feeling on April 18 when Butser [Hill] was but a great jump away over hollow land early in morning and sky all blue but one white cloud.'

63 *The Huxter*

See *Berg FNB* 77, 24 Aug. 1914: 'Ledbury—met a huckster.' (During a holiday spent with the family of Robert Frost.)

## 65  *Song* [1]

The poet's comment on the poem in his letter to Eleanor Farjeon (28 Apr. 1915) is half-ironic: 'But I promise you I am under a thick cloud of Marlborough mostly, tho I wrote a sort of a song in it; . . . [the song follows]. Does it make you larf?'

The same day Thomas replied to the first long letter he had received from Robert Frost after his return to the U.S.A. (Frost's letter arrived in early April 1915, just before W. H. Davies spent a few days at Steep.) He wrote: 'You're a literary man like me. Do you know I go on with verses to the detriment of Marlborough: take the 2 best hours out of my morning with I am afraid rather poetical things sometimes. Did you think it might become a habit?'

## 67  *Melancholy*

*2 fever*: see letter to Eleanor Farjeon dated 28 Apr. 1915 (*TLFY*, p. 131): 'I was rather ill for 4 days with a chill or I would have written—a chill and a boil together.' Thomas spent the next four days from Monday (26 Apr.) to Thursday (29 Apr.) working at the British Museum on his *Marlborough*, and staying again with his parents at Balham.

*9-10* See *Berg FNB* 80, undated but after 18 Apr. 1915:

> ~~Dripping water sweet as dulcimer~~
> In the wind
> I thought I heard the cuckoo all day long
> 40 years had crimsoned his cheeks with pain and pleasure

## 68  *Tonight*

*1* There is no evidence to suggest reasons for the change of name from 'Margaret' (in the early manuscripts) to 'Harry'.

## 69  *April*

*12* See Thomas's letter to Frost dated 3 May 1915:

> I find I can't write. Re-reading Rupert Brooke and putting a few things together about him [Thomas's article 'Rupert Brooke' in *The English Review*, 20, pp. 325-8, June 1915] have rather messed me up and there's Marlborough behind and Marlborough before. . . . Are the children at school now? Or are you still 'neglecting' them? God bless them all. By the way, there was a beautiful return of sun yesterday after a misty moisty morning, and everything smelt wet and warm and cuckoos called and I found myself with nothing to say but 'God bless it'. I laughed a little as I came over the field, thinking about the 'it' in 'God bless it'. . . .
>
> P.S. Here is [V. Locke] Ellis very elderly and masterly about my verses, not ~~troubling to say~~ finding one to say he likes, but seeing the 'elements of poetry'. The rhythm is too rough

and not obvious enough. He wants to talk them over. I don't. Well, I feel sure I'm old
enough not to know better, though I don't profess to know how good or bad it may be.

*14  Emily*: possibly a half-memory of Emily Bottomley. See Letter 148 to Gordon
Bottomley, dated 6 May 1915: 'I have been wondering many times about you
all, your Mother, Aunt Sarah, Mrs. Burton, and You and Emily with those four
points to her compass. I hope she isn't tired out.'

## 69–71 *April, The Glory*, and *July*

See *Berg FNB* 80, undated, between 18 Apr. and 23 May 1915:

> As we met—the nightingale sang
> As we loved ——————————
> As we parted ——————the same.
>
> Coming to ask forgiveness for something I had not noticed
> Smiling with a half-certainty to be forgiven.
> 'God bless it' was all I could say and laughed to find
> no other words.
> Now it is when Kate comes to me ——
>                 God bless her
> Nightingale's tsoo tsoo tsooed
>                 Turned in tears back
>
> Dog that barked so hoarse and old by Luff's house (near old
> farmyard and trees) and also by river and rother under echoing banks
> The happy seeming short lived things we do not understand
> Nightingale[,] aspern joy of life and grief of dark
> I exult and then I despair in beauty that bears no
> correspondence in any strength or wisdom known to me
> ~~down in the val~~
> Doves invite to something sweeter than truer
> How swift time passes when nothing is
>                 ————
> In Time ——— still hour after hour
> Filled to content with what ring doves say
>     ~~I thought the above worth thinking of saying~~.

## 72 *The Chalk Pit*

See *Berg FNB* 80, dated between 23 May and 2 June 1915:

> A girl of 20 with a boy's brown face
> Thick eyebrows glinting eyes:
>                 You have said enough
> Oh yes.

*2 June 1915*

> The smell like honeycomb of mugwort dull
> and brown hair, brown as a thrush or as a nut
> the frizzled water over sun all *stones*

The way light is there before you in a dark cupboard as soon as you open it.

*Berg FNB* 80, undated, between 25 Mar. and 23 May 1915: 'Did something once happen there at the bend of the road Round the chalk pit old.'

    See also Thomas's essay 'Chalk Pits', printed in *The Last Sheaf*, pp. 27–37, which contains many prose adumbrations of this poem. (The renewal of correspondence with Frost may well have occasioned Thomas's return to the use of older, prose material as the basis of new verse.)

*18* See *The Last Sheaf*, p. 31: 'They have names of their own; often they are dells, such as Stubridge Dell, or Slade Dell. . . . These islands are attractive largely, I think, because they suggest fragments of primaeval forest that have been left untouched by the plough on account of their roughness.'

*43* An echo of many wry self-portraits that are in Thomas's prose writings.

*44 orts*: then a colloquial form of 'noughts'.

*47–52* These lines are based on memories of his open-air courtship of Helen Noble in and around London, Wiltshire, and Oxford.

*56–8* See 'The Friend of the Blackbird' in *The Last Sheaf*, p. 211: 'He did not forget the trees—"those tethered dreamers, standing on one leg like Indian mystics". With them also he felt the same community, as though more rarely and in a way not to be spoken except by putting out his hand to touch their bark and leaves.'

## 73 *Fifty Faggots*

This poem, untitled, is part of a letter sent to Robert Frost from London, dated 15 May 1915: 'This is the end of I hope my last week's reading for "Marlborough" . . . One of my reliefs in this week's work was to write these lines founded on carrying up 50 bunts (short faggots of thin and thick brushwood mixed) and putting them against our hedge.' After the poem, Thomas asks, 'Are they [the lines] *north* of Boston only?' *North of Boston* was the second volume of Frost's poetry published in England and favourably reviewed by Thomas (see *GB*, p. 233). The phrase 'north of Boston' occurs frequently in his letters to Frost: it is shorthand for poems based on rural incidents presented in simulated colloquial language.

*15* Thomas included Webster's 'Dirge' ('Call for the robin-redbreast and the wren') in *TE*, p. 74.

## 74 *Sedge-Warblers* [Cancelled version]

In a letter to Robert Frost, dated 23 May 1915, Thomas wrote: 'It seemed I had dried up, owing to Marlborough, but I have done a thing today. I shall send [it] if I find time to copy it. It came of a Sunday with no work but a cycle ride with Bronwen [his elder daughter]. It is devilish like habit, but I am all rules and evasions.' Earlier in the letter Thomas wrote: 'But it has been pleasant walking up and down, too [i.e. from Steep village to his study up on Wick Green]. Such a lovely May it is, hot and with a bustling wind.' He added a postscript the next day: 'There are a good many moments when I feel there is hardly anybody that matters except God in Gloucestershire or any other county. I have been very impatient with people lately and yet sorry they have drifted off.'

See *Berg FNB* 80:

*23 May 1915*: beyond Warnford . . .

Water crowfoot and marigolds iris leaf and clear swift combing water but no nymph only the sedge warblers in millions more continuous than earth and clearer than sweetest voice singing sweetest *words* I know, tho' often grating or shrill and always jerky and spasmodic with nice sweet gentle iterations and 3 or 4 together or in fours.

> Long ago it would have borne a nymph
>    — cloudless clear sail
> Now it reflects the chestnut petals from the distant park
> She could
> Love all day long and never hate or tire
> the best of May
> Buttercups brighter than brass
>    — soft.

## 77 *Words*

During June 1915, after finishing *Marlborough*, Thomas had spent some time re-reading Frost's *North of Boston* while he was writing his article on Rupert Brooke. He then set off on a cycling tour and spent three days with W. J. Haines 'cycling about and talking of you [Frost]'. Before leaving Steep, Thomas had written a long letter to Frost about his own verse. 'Words' and 'The Word' (Poem 78) should be seen in the context of this period of stock-taking which ended with his enlistment a fortnight later.

## 78 *The Word*

See Berg, *FNB* 80, undated, after 2 June 1915:

> Things forgotten—
> I have forgotten the names of the stars, the big above the little
> and to one side—and dates of wars etc.
>    But I remember
> Those little copses of blackbird and nettles. bramble where
> a man might hide  For ever dead or alive.

See Berg *FNB* 61: '28 January 1913. Story of man remembering little sweet woodbird he only heard once as a child.'

## 79 *Under the Wood*

See *Berg FNB* 80, undated, after 2 June 1915: 'Lazy keeper in col under woods [above ~~wood hanger~~]—smokes and has one green shrivelled stoat, he killed ages ago when trees were young—never shoots now.' This sentence is in the middle of prose notes used for Poem 80.

## 80 *Haymaking*

Thomas devotes four pages of notes to this poem in *Berg FNB* 80, undated, but after 2 June 1915:

[p. 11]    Park mead of thin grass mown by white priest or grove of low squat oaks and
long grass and men under—a solitary yew—also on the slopes—wych hazel and
flowering elder—a rick in midfield—tosser idle—men lean on rakes—old
fashioned as Crome or Constable.

    How old it is. I seem to see it now as some one long years hence will see it in
a picture.

        Hot air has a kernel of cold
[~~The hot air has a kernel sweet of cold~~]

[p. 12]    The hunchbacked woman that roots daisies up in Salisbury Close.
honeysuckle and white musk rose in lanes of Sherfield English
by the mill.
Water racing white and tossing at foot of mill fall in Compton
Chamberlain, happier in sun than any crowd of children pouring
out of school.

                           clearer, no
Old tracks down the Downs no ^ straighter, than wind strikes on
the sea.
Lazy keeper . . . never shoots now. [See Note to Poem 79.]

[p. 13]    hawthorn and ivy intertwined—and inseparable in Forest of Dean,
with low bracken and tall foxglove between.
the thunder sky's dark blue maw
Clean Cotswolds with dark winds and pink stone towns and villages steep.
The fluster of the blood adown her throat
The little house in the great trees

    After thunder and night rain, glorious hot bright fresh morning with
clouds like gods bathing in the sea before they made the world.

    (Words light as gossamer, Honey sweet, precious as gold and strong as steel.
As the hills are old.) [See Poem 76, 'Words'.]

    In thunderstorm when we hurry home the ducks set out for a walk
in a line along the road to reach the hollow that will be pools.
The little fine antennae of the hollies
The fallen fir cones stand up in the heat.

[p. 14]    [This page is cancelled with a diagonal line]:

> The fiery air had a kernel sweet of cold
> After the thunder far away had ~~rolled~~ stopped
> And in the quietness (guileless) the clouds overhead
> Like the first gods before they made the world
> And joyous bathed in Homer's sea
> A lighter wind in the silent grass said Yes.
>
> With the autumn of the hollies that falls in June
> The perfect smooth white empty road was strewn
> And fir cones standing up stiff on their head
> The — fir stood close under great elms
> ____
> The millpond water racing white and tossing
> Crystal rejoieed [*above* ~~with happiness~~] more in the sun than any crowd
> Of children running out of school aloud
> ____
> And in the little copses where a sleeper
> Alive or dead might
> Might lie for ever lost the nettle creeper
> And garden warblers sang unceasingly
> What never then ~~in their~~ shrieked in the fierce glee
> The swifts.

[p. 15]    Older than Clare and work was the Moreland [*sic*] and Crome.

There follow twelve lines of a first sketch of Poem 81, 'A Dream', and then:

> bathing in stormless sea
> In beauty and in divine ~~happiness~~ Beauty.


## 81  *A Dream* [*Sonnet* 1]

See Thomas's letter to Frost from 13 Rusham Rd., Balham, dated 22 July 1915. After giving some reasons for his enlistment on 14 July, Thomas wrote: 'A month or two [ago] I dreamt we were walking near Ledington but we lost one another in a strange place and I woke saying to myself "Somehow someday I shall be here again" which I made the last lines of some verses.'

*Berg FNB* 80, undated, after 2 June 1915, has two draft versions of this poem; the second version is very close to the printed text except for alternative versions of l. 14:

> ·Saying 'Someday, somehow, I shall be here again
> Saying 'I shall be here, someday, somehow, again.

Thomas recorded many dreams in his various notebooks, all carefully worked over as if for publication, often with clear indications of their source in waking experience. When this poem was written Thomas was gradually reaching a decision not to follow Frost and settle in New Hampshire. On his own admission, the dream firmly recalls his long visit to Frost in August 1914. After that visit

Thomas went to South Wales. *Berg MS 64B9046* contains *Penderyn*, a holograph essay, dated 6 Sept. 1914 by Thomas, which includes a careful description of the underground river course and the waterfalls at Ystradfellte seen during a long walk from Neath to Penderyn and the Brecknock Beacons. The following sentence from the essay suggests ll. 2–7: 'There was now no valley, and not a yard of level ground between these hills. The river in one place ran black underground, and in another danced down a quarter mile of cascades, white as milk.'

Some time between the late autumn of 1914 and his enlistment, Thomas collected and labelled all his field notebooks, perhaps while in search of material that resembled the incidents and encounters in Frost's poems *North of Boston*. The essay *Penderyn* is in the usual penultimate stage prior to publication; opposite the title and original date, Thomas has added 'not copied yet, March 1915'.

In *Berg FNB 80*, on the page after one dated 23 May 1915, Thomas gives a numbered list of topics:

(1) She came then, but she never came again
(2) The first peacock
(3) See back [i.e. the last pages of the notebook with a series of brief entries dated from 1 Jan. 1915 to 2 May 1915. The final entry, while he was a soldier training in London, is dated 7 Sept. 1915.]
(4) The stone the carthorse kicks against so oft. [See Poem 82]
(5) Sometimes someday I shall be here again (waking from dream of deep pool. Full of [?inn]
[?white] water revolving and plunging—dream of Frost too and a walk to this.)
I woke with this line of farewell to the place.
(6) [The first entry referred to in Note to Poem 82.]

The relationship between Frost and Thomas will be fully documented by me in the *Special Edward Thomas Number* of *Poetry Wales*, Spring 1978.


## 82  *The Brook*

The child in the poem is the poet's younger daughter, Myfanwy. The day after writing it, Sunday, 11 June 1915, Thomas wrote to Frost about his decision to visit London on Wednesday for a medical examination prior to enlisting in The Artists' Rifles.

See *Berg FNB 80* for three relevant entries:
(1) Undated, between 23 May and 2 June 1915:

> Not since ~~the horse~~
> The horseman and the horse in silver shoes
> That lie now in the Bramdean tumulus
> Ceased riding on the Downs
> That sleep within [*above* lie within] the barrow ~~by the Dean~~
> on the heath
>
> past rode
> Ceased riding on the Downs.

(2) Page 9, dated 2 June 1915:

> The smell like honeycomb of
> mugwort dull

(3) Page 10, undated, after 2 June 1915:

> Nobody's been here before says Baba [Myfanwy] paddling
> in sandy brook—so she thinks.

> Mellow the blackbird, tart the thrush
> The bat hangs head down in the barn

> And this heavy elder scent like a rose
> And the rose scent like a memory
> Where the dark water bursts straight out into the world

> The rodent flycatcher grey on the fence.

## 83 *Aspens*

See Thomas's letter to Eleanor Farjeon (*TLFY*, pp. 152-3), dated 21 July 1915: 'About "Aspens" you missed just the turn that I thought essential. *I* was the aspen. "We" meant the trees and I with my dejected shyness. Does that clear it up, or do you think in rereading it that I have not emphasised it enough?'

*22* See note to Poem 30, p. 388.

## 84 *The Mill-Water*

See *Berg FNB* 80, undated, after 2 June 1915: 'Mill full sound—heard by those alone who are thinking and stop suddenly—and by those who watch long—so that they seem to feel with all who ever listened to it when mill was there.'

## 85 *For these* [*Prayer*]

Thomas began this poem on the day before he was passed medically fit for enlistment, and finished it the next day. It is referred to as 'the prayer' in his letter to Eleanor Farjeon, dated 15 July 1915—whence the new editorial title.

  See *Berg FNB* 80, undated, after 2 June 1915, for a cancelled early approach to this poem:

> I don't wish for an acre of land
> But for content and something to be contented with or else
> If I could live long enough to get content with what I have
>                          the hills
> An acre of land between ~~Cutts~~ and the sea and near them
> both or some hilltop
> A station for the herald Mercury

Garden whose sunflowers every one
Was fit to be the sign of the rising sun.

I do not wish for them, but not too late
And not too little, for content but
Something to be contented with perhaps.

## 86  *Digging* [2]

This was the first poem after his enlistment and was written at his parents' home
in Balham while he was off-duty with a strained tendon. See the letter to Eleanor
Farjeon (dated 21 July 1915 in *TLFY*, pp. 153-4) which contains the first draft
of the poem: '. . . I have been perspiring these six hours over ten lines which
perhaps are not right yet. But if you would type them for me I could see them
better.'

4  These references follow directly from his recently completed *Life of the Duke
of Marlborough*.

See *Berg FNB* 80, undated, but before 25 Mar. 1915, immediately after brief
entries about Poems 21 and 27 and before entry on Poem 45:

Finding an old pipe and one of mine in garden. Someone
will assuredly find mine when I am not.
He created the elephant.

## 89  *October*

This was the first poem written since Thomas's first week as a soldier. His
training was mainly in London (where he was billeted on his parents), with
musketry practice at High Beech, Essex, where he later moved his family (see
*TLFY*, pp. 164-72). After Eleanor Farjeon had typed some copies of 'October'
he replied in an undated letter (*TLFY*, p. 169):

I expect you are right about the rhymes, most of them. The original version was in blank
verse, but quite different. Hasn't Bronwen taught you tormentil, the tiny yellow flower
in short hill grass, a flat buttercup or avens with rather separate petals. Tormentilla it is.
The accent is on the second syllable which doesn't (as I see it) affect the merit of the line
whatever it may be; I mean doesn't tell against it. I suppose the influence of High Beech
and the Artists ought to be clearer. I am going to slightly better conditions, but don't
expect to write till I am disabled again. The knee is now well.

See first entry in *Berg FNB* 80, dated 1 Jan. 1915, after a series of nature notes:
'A mood long blackened and obscured by the name of melancholy.'

## 90  *There's nothing like the sun*

See *Berg FNB* 80, 1 Nov. 1915: 'Sweet as last damsons on spangled tree when
November starling imitates the swallow in sunny interval between rain and all

is still and dripping.' And 16 Nov. 1915: 'There's nothing like the sun in January—.'

## 91 *The Thrush*

The poem was probably written after reading Gordon Bottomley's poem 'Eager Spring' in *TE* (which appeared in late 1915). See *GB*, pp. 255-7, especially Letter 160: 'In case you can attend to an anthology I am sending mine with your thrush in it. It comes with love to you and Emily.'

See three scattered references to thrush song among many in the notebooks:

(1) *Berg FNB* 64: '8 July 1913. Rusham Road [Balham]: 6-7.15 a.m. one thrush hammering away at one triple cry, message or whatever anyone else likes.'

(2) *Berg FNB* 80: on the right-hand side: '1 February 1915: How I noticed the one thrush near the tip of poplar 250 yards beyond Nightingale Lane in opening of Rusham Road—he was singing, the only one.'

On the left-hand side:

> I hear you alone and see
> You alone at the end of the lane
> Near the bare poplar's tip
> Singing continuously.

(3) *Berg FNB* 80; after an entry dated 26 Nov. 1915:

> Thrush
> When winter's ahead
> What can you see in November
> That you see in April
> When Winter's dead,

## 92 *Liberty*

The Keatsian echoes in the poem could be amplified by reading Thomas's comments on Keats's Odes (see his *Keats*, pp. 53-8) and character (especially *Keats*, pp. 74-5). 'Liberty' is referred to in his letter to Robert Frost dated 6 Dec. 1915: 'I don't want to read anything. On the other hand as soon as I get really free with nothing else before me to do I incline to write. I have written two things here [Hare Hall Camp] or rather three, but one was just rhyming on.—I am always just a little more outside things than most of the others, without being made to feel so at all acutely. They aren't surprised, whether I come in or stay out of a group.' (The third poem, 'rhyming on', probably refers to 'The Thrush'.)

See *Berg FNB* 80, undated entry, after 7 Sept. and before 1 Nov. 1915:

> The moonlight lies on the grass as white as frost beyond
> the brink of the tall elm shadow.

The worst of all is
~~When nothing matters~~
The worst of all is doing nothing when There's nothing to do and
you are only free For what you do not like and you like nothing.
                                                    (See later) [Thomas]

The moonless night died to a sunless day
                        a light
A little light that for hours you can see nothing but itself

See also an undated entry, after 1 Nov. and before 16 Nov. 1915:

If I could have all such hours in a pile and dip in and take a handful and be rich or sweep
all away for ever I should be rich to be so poor.

## 93 [*This is no case of petty right or wrong*]

6 See Thomas's letter to Eleanor Farjeon, dated 7 Jan. 1916 (*TLFY*, p. 180):
'I am not sure that "love true" [l. 6] is a mistake, but perhaps "love I will not"
is, and I suggest

                        Philosophers
        ~~Can see~~ I hate not Germans, nor grow hot
        With love of English, to please newspapers.

But perhaps it won't do. I am so busy now.'

Although *Bod* gives the place and date of composition as Steep, 26 Dec. 1915,
the letter quoted above to Eleanor Farjeon continues: 'I did write the couplets
[ll. 20-6] at Steep, but the others some weeks ago here [Hare Hall Camp]. Helen
won't like them a bit and I kept them by me undecided. I hope you are right.'
Actually Helen liked the poem when she saw it and urged him to send it to editors.

The mood behind the poem—almost a justification of his decision to enlist—
is reflected in a later letter to Gordon Bottomley (*GB*, no. 161, dated 11 Feb.
1916). But it is even more explicit in the following extracts from a letter sent to
Robert Frost, dated 2 Jan. 1916:

Yesterday I got up to London (it being Saturday) for the day and saw Monro and Davies
. . . In town I saw my father too, and he made me very sick. . . . Nothing much happened.
We argued about the war and he showed that his real feeling when he is not trying to be
nice and comfortable is one of contempt. I know what contempt is and partly what I
suffered was from the reminder that I had probably made Helen feel exactly the same.
I came more readily back to camp than ever before. I shall recover; but it makes a difference.

The conscious literary echoes and tone of the poem reflect his choice of extracts
for Section VI ('Great Ones') of *TE*, pp. 133-54. Thomas had made similar points
in his 1914 article, 'England', reprinted in *The Last Sheaf*, especially p. 111:

I believe the man who thought it a 'quaint' idea to love England would feel very much as
I do about these passages and about Walton altogether. I believe that England means
something like this to most of us; that all ideas of England are developed, spun out, from
such a centre into something large or infinite, solid or aëry, according to each man's nature
and capacity; that England is a system of vast circumferences circling round the minute
neighbouring points of home.

See *Berg FNB* 77: '26 August 1914. Wet day—with a third moon bright and almost orange low down clear of cloud and I thought of men eastward seeing it at the same moment. It seems foolish to have loved England up to now without knowing it could perhaps be ravaged and I could and perhaps *would* do nothing to prevent it.'

Two Christmas letters to his Californian aunt also illustrate Thomas's long wrestle with himself about the war:

(1) dated 23 Nov. 1914:

> The war must probably last many months, more than a year, longer . . . I can't imagine that as men are at present, and as I imagine they will long remain, a nation is much use that is not capable of this violent folly, when the body and whatever of the mind can work with the body prevails and boasts itself. But I should like to avoid too much of this strain because it is not the strain of the men who are fighting or going to fight, but rather of morbid people in whom their balance and fusion of mind and body is impossible, and who admire frantically what is impossible to themselves.

(2) dated 21 Nov. 1915:

> The men about me never talk of the war for more than a moment or two at a time, though most of them will be in it before long. I really hope my turn will come and that I shall see what it really is and come out of it with my head and most of my limbs. Then I may yet go to America and begin afresh and this time will not have been wasted.

There are three earlier relevant entries in *Berg FNB* 79 (dated by Thomas 'from October–December 1914'):

> The war national but as yet dark and chaotic in brain—e.g. no good war poems early in Napoleonic Wars. Some writers can go on with old work but no reason why they should at once be able to admit war into their subject matter. Poetry excepting cheapest kind shows this dark chaotic character.
>
> People expressing all sorts of views and trumping up old canting catchwords, but not yet the compact essential real truth to this occasion alone.
>
> Statesman may say 'No price too high when honour and freedom are at stake' etc. But can't be translated into poetry.

> *England*
> Where a woman and child can cross safe.
> The kernel is yourself and your country the nut—her life depends on the nut.

> *War.* 31 October 1914—morning after Turkey's declaration of War. The young don't feel their responsibility and are afraid of their skins (said Salter the Post-man).
> (I know what I was like at their age.)

Finally, see *Berg FNB* 80, dated 26 Nov. 1915:

> This is no case of little right or wrong
> That statesman and philosopher
> Can see. For it involves our love. I do not know and
> hardly more I care
> But do know that bone of her bone [I am?]
>
> rain that smokes along the wind athwart the wood
>
> Cry God save England else we too will sink
>
>> live with
> And shall be [clothed and?] and fed like animals.

## 94 *Rain*

For an earlier, and deceptively similar, prose account of Thomas's response to the rain, composed at Steep during August and September 1911, see *The Icknield Way*, pp. 280–3:

I lay awake listening to the rain, and at first it was as pleasant to my ear and my mind as it had long been desired; but before I fell asleep it had become a majestic and finally a terrible thing, instead of a sweet sound and symbol. It was accusing and trying me and passing judgment. Long I lay still under the sentence, listening to the rain, and then at last listening to words which seemed to be spoken by a ghostly double beside me. He was muttering: The all-night rain puts out summer like a torch. In the heavy, black rain falling straight from invisible, dark sky to invisible, dark earth the heat of summer is annihilated, the splendour is dead, the summer is gone. The midnight rain buries it away where it has buried all sound but its own. I am alone in the dark still night, and my ear listens to the rain piping in the gutters and roaring softly in the trees of the world. Even so will the rain fall darkly upon the grass over the grave when my ears can hear it no more. I have been glad of the sound of rain, and wildly sad of it in the past; but that is all over as if it had never been; my eye is dull and my heart beating evenly and quietly; I stir neither foot nor hand; I shall not be quieter when I lie under the wet grass and the rain falls, and I of less account than the grass. The summer is gone, and never can it return. There will never be any summer any more, and I am weary of everything. I stay because I am too weak to go. I crawl on because it is easier than to stop. I put my face to the window. There is nothing out there but the blackness and sound of rain. Neither when I shut my eyes can I see anything. I am alone. Once I heard through the rain a bird's questioning watery cry— once only and suddenly. It seemed content, and the solitary note brought up against me the order of nature, all its beauty, exuberance, and everlastingness like an accusation. I am not a part of nature. I am alone. There is nothing else in my world but my dead heart and brain within me and the rain without. Once there was summer, and a great heat and splendour over the earth terrified me and asked me what I could show that was worthy of such an earth. It smote and humiliated me, yet I had eyes to behold it, and I prostrated myself, and by adoration made myself worthy of the splendour. Was I not once blind to the splendour because there was something within me equal to itself? What was it? Love . . . a name! . . . a word! . . . less than the watery question of the bird out in the rain. The rain has drowned the splendour. Everything is drowned and dead, all that was once lovely and alive in the world, all that had once been alive and was memorable though dead is now dung for a future that is infinitely less than the falling dark rain. For a moment the mind's eye and ear pretend to see and hear what the eye and ear themselves once knew with delight. The rain denies. There is nothing to be seen or heard, and there never was. Memory, the last chord of the lute, is broken. The rain has been and will be for ever over the earth. There never was anything but the dark rain. Beauty and strength are as nothing to it. Eyes could not flash in it.

I have been lying dreaming until now, and now I have awakened, and there is still nothing but the rain. I am alone. The unborn is not more weak or more ignorant, and like the unborn I wait and wait, knowing neither what has been nor what is to come, because of the rain, which is, has been, and must be. The house is still and silent, and those small noises that make me start are only the imagination of the spirit or they are the rain. There is only the rain for it to feed on and to crawl in. The rain swallows it up as the sea does its own foam. I will lie still and stretch out my body and close my eyes. My breath is all that has been spared by the rain, and that comes softly and at long intervals, as if it were trying to hide itself from the rain. I feel that I am so little I have crept away into a corner and been forgotten by the rain. All else has perished except me and the rain. There is no room for anything in the world but the rain. It alone is great and strong. It alone knows joy. It chants monotonous praise of the order of nature, which I have disobeyed or slipped out of. I have done evilly and weakly, and I have left undone. Fool! you never were alive. Lie still. Stretch out yourself like foam on a wave, and think no more of good or evil. There was no good and no evil. There was life and there was death, and you chose. Now there is neither life nor death, but only the rain. Sleep as all things, past, present, and future, lie still and sleep, except the rain, the heavy, black rain falling straight through the air that was once a sea of life. That was a dream only. The truth is that the rain falls for ever and I am melting into it. Black and monotonously sounding is the midnight and solitude of the rain. In a little while or in an age—for it is all one—I shall know the full truth of the words I used to love, I knew not why, in my days of nature, in the days before the rain: 'Blessed are the dead that the rain rains on.'

The stresses undergone by Thomas while composing *The Icknield Way* are fully documented in *GB*, pp. 208-21.


## 95 *Song* [2]

As a Lance-Corporal Instructor in map-reading at this time Thomas had fewer week-end leaves at home and more daily responsibilities, but ample leisure to write in Camp at week-ends. See his letter to Robert Frost of 16 Jan. 1916: 'Half the men are away this weekend, and the rest are out with friends, and I have had a lot of time to myself—which always tempts me to write and sometimes I do.' And in another letter to Frost of 30 Jan. 1916:

> I got home a week ago for 24 hours. Now this weekend has to be spent in camp with no work to do except look after the hut while my superior is away. These are the worst days. The only real cure is to get quite alone and write. I can sometimes get the hut empty and write. Then I sometimes write in the train going home late. I must send you one or two recent verses. 'Lob' and 'Words' are to appear in a big hotchpotch called 'Form' in March. Otherwise I keep out of print.

See, too, the following extract from a letter to his wife, probably written on 24 Jan. 1916: 'Fancy your thinking I might have someone in view in those verses beginning "The clouds that are so light". Fancy your being pleased at the idea. Well, perhaps you wouldn't be, if there really were someone, in which case I would hardly write verses, I think.'


## 96 *Roads*

*33* A reference to the Welsh Roman Road called 'Sarn Helen'. See his letter to Eleanor Farjeon, dated 24 Jan. 1916:

> 16 verses I see it makes. Helen is the lady in the Mabinogion, the Welsh lady who married Maxen the Emperor and gave her name to the great old mountain roads—Sarn Helen they are all marked on the maps. Do you remember the 'Dream of Maxen'? She is known to mythologists as one of the travelling goddesses of the dusk. But perhaps I don't convey much in my 16 verses.

Thomas expands the point, too, in the letter to his wife quoted above (Poem 95):

> I like some of it a good deal. That Helen is more real than the lady in the 4 verses [of Song [2]]. Oh, you needn't think of another lady. There would have to be 2 to make a love affair and I am only one. Nobody but you would ever be likely to respond as I wished. I don't like to think anybody but I could respond to you. If you turned to anybody else I should come to an end immediately.

There are numerous references to roads, and paths, and long walks in the extant Field Note Books. See especially *Berg FNB* 53, containing notes of a series of cycle journeys with his son, Merfyn; the notebook is headed 'Marlboro', Pewsey, Amesbury, Salisbury, Tisbury' and dated 1 May 1911:

> *11 May, Avebury.* I never saw such a village for paths etc. round about, all over a space of about a mile—a good book might be written of these paths alone, a very good book. The crosses might have been made on purpose to exorcise the Druid's ghosts. Children of 8 or 9 (girls) gathering cowslips silently, bending, and unbending, in field just before I entered Avebury and they reminded me of the children in Chaucer's Prioress' Tale (p. 86. ll. 1688-9) for one sang a hymn like a song.

This was one of the notebooks used for *The Icknield Way* (1913).


## 98  *February Afternoon* [*Sonnet 2*]

The mood of this poem is to some extent explained in two letters. One is to Frost, dated 21 Feb. 1916: 'I have had a bit of a holiday lately. I took a chill somewhat and had to take to bed in my father's house.' The other, dated 6 Feb. 1916, is to his wife: 'Well I can't write more. I am only fit to lie and listen to Mother reading Revelations.'

See *Berg FNB* 80: '*4 February 1915.* Sometimes dozens of starlings—separately in hedge and in oaks of meadow behind are talking at same time—the sweetest sound, democratic crowd imaginable. The sweetest democracy imaginable. Thrushes sing till after 5.15.'


## 99  [*P. H. T.*]

The relationship between father and son was a difficult one but not as implacable as this poem suggests. (See *Edward Thomas* (*Writers of Wales*), p. 58.) During his first seven or eight months as a soldier training in and around London, Thomas spent a great deal of time at his parents' home. This poem was written there when the poet was sick with a chill (see note to Poem 98); a little earlier he had decided to avoid his father for a time because of their opposed attitudes to the war (see note to Poem 93) and, I suspect, Thomas's refusal to take a commission. This temporary breach was probably exacerbated by the father's attitude to his son's poetry. The poet's nephew (Mr. E. E. Thomas), the elder son of Julian Thomas, has kindly allowed me to quote the following extract from a notebook diary kept by his father during 1914-18: 'Tuesday, 23 March 1915 . . . I read out a score of Edwy's poetry to Mother and Maud [J. T.'s wife] the other night. Father calls them pure piffle and says no one will publish them. He may be right as to the last part of the sentence.' Julian was very close to his eldest brother and at a Fabian Summer School in late 1918 he read his brother's poems to a group that included G. B. Shaw and C. E. M. Joad. Many of P. H. Thomas's grandchildren and one grand-nephew have told me that they regard this picture as a partial and incomplete one.

## 100 [*These things that poets said*]

Thomas's *The Tenth Muse* (a slightly modified form of Chapter 8 from his *Feminine Influence on the Poets*) was reissued in 1916 and a re-reading of its introductory paragraph may have prompted this poem. See *The Tenth Muse*, p. 8: 'Their [women's] chief direct influence has been exerted by the stimulation of desire—desire to possess not only them but other known and unknown things deemed necessary to that perfection of beauty and happiness which love proposes. It is a desire of impossible things which the poet alternately assuages and arouses again by poetry, in himself and in us.' The relationship between love and poetry is developed more fully on p. 2 of the abandoned typescript of *Ecstasy* in *Berg* 73B6771 (fourteen typescript pages left unfinished in September 1913).

## 101 [*M. E. T.*]

This poem about Thomas's mother, a companion piece to Poem 99 ['P. H. T.'], was written at the end of a short illness spent at his parents' home. (See R. P. Eckert, *Edward Thomas*, pp. 248-9, and *Edward Thomas* (*Writers of Wales*), pp. 58-9.) The close relationship between mother and son is borne out by Thomas's letter to Robert Frost from 13 Rusham Road, Balham, after his enlistment (dated 22 July 1915): 'There is no one to keep me here [England] except my mother. She might come too. But I couldn't in this present mess pack up and get born again in New Hampshire. I couldn't have before I took the king's shilling.'

An earlier picture of his mother (probably written between 1913 and 1914) emerges from the poet's fragment of autobiography, *The Childhood of Edward Thomas*:

> My mother I can hardly see save as she is now while I am writing. I cannot see her but I can summon up her presence. She is plainest to me not quite dressed, in white bodice and petticoat, her arms and shoulders rounded and creamy smooth. My affection for her was leavened with lesser likings and with admiration. I liked the scent of her fresh warm skin and supposed it unique. Her straight nose and chin made a profile that for years formed my standard. No hair was so beautiful to me as hers was, light golden brown hair, long and rippling. Her singing at fall of night, especially if we were alone together, soothed and fascinated me, as though it had been divine, at once the mightiest and the softest sound in the world. [pp. 18-19]

> But I liked to please my mother and keep undisturbed the love that was between us. I sometimes did little unexpected kind things out of my tenderness for her, and was always

glad to be the one to take up tea for her if she was unwell, and so on, or to help her with the housework when she was left servantless. But with her as with everyone I was deceitful and had dread of being caught doing what I ought not to do. It was a great and frequent dread. For I felt that most things a boy liked doing annoyed some elder or another; that to annoy an elder was the essence of wrong. My solution was to try not to annoy at the same time that I was doing almost as I liked. Deceit and dread increased rapidly. [p. 76]

## 102 *The Unknown*

For Edward Thomas's lifelong concern with the ideals of 'love' and 'beauty'—which he shared with Gordon Bottomley—see 'The Fountain' in his collection of stories, *Rest and Unrest* (1910), pp. 143–4:

> As a boy it was of such a being that I used to think—though my imagination was not energetic enough to body it forth quite clearly—when I felt, in loneliest places among the woods or clouds, that my foot-falls had scared something shy, beautiful, and divine. And more than so, she was akin to the spirit abroad on many days that had awed or harassed me with loveliness—to the spirit on the dewy clovers, in the last star that hung like a bird of light scattering gold and silver from her wings in the cold blue and gloomy rose of the dawn; to the spirit in mountain or forest waters, in many unstained rivers, in all places where Nature had stung me with a sense of her own pure force, pure and without pity. . . .
>
> These were the fancies of the moment. She was in sight for less than a minute as I went up from the sea over the moor, and when I turned in one of its hollows she had disappeared and I saw nothing but sea and sky, which were as one.

These ideas are further explored in Poem 103.

## 103 *Celandine*

This poem was written after Thomas had received a letter from Frost on his birthday, 3 Mar. 1916. See his reply to Frost, dated 5 Mar. 1916:

> I have been restless lately. Partly the annoyance of my promotion [to Corporal] being delayed. Partly the rain and the long hours indoors. Partly my 10 days chill. Then there has been measles in the camp for 6 weeks and now we have it and are isolated and denied our leave this week, which includes my birthday when I meant to be at Steep . . . This should only improve what you condemn as my fastidious taste in souls. Yet soul is a word I feel I can't have used for years and years. Anyhow here I have to like people because they are more my sort than the others, although I realise at certain times they are not my sort at all and will vanish away after the war. What almost completes the illusion is that I can't help talking to them as if they were friends.
>
> Partly what made me restless was the desire to write, without the power. It lasted 5 or 6 weeks till yesterday I rhymed some. Your talking of epic and play rather stirred me. I shall be careful not to *indulge* in a spring run of lyrics, I had better try again to make other people speak. I suppose I take it easily, especially now when it is partly an indulgence. —I wish you would send some of yours without bargaining.

## 104 'Home' [3]

The background to this poem is filled out by Thomas's letter to Frost (dated 21 May 1916) about his visit to the theatre to see Bottomley's play, *Wife of King Lear*:

> Bottomley and his wife I just had a word with. I was with a young artist named Paul Nash who has just joined us as a map reader. He is a change from the two schoolmasters I see most of. He is wonderful at finding birds' nests. There is another artist, too, aged 24, a Welshman, absolutely a perfect Welshman, kind, simple, yet all extremes, and rather unreal and incredible except in his admirations—he admires his wife and Rembrandt, for example. I am really lucky to have such a crowd of people always round and these two or three nearer! You might guess from 'Home' how much nearer.

See also note to Poem 103.

## 106-9 *Household Poems*

For these four poems about his family see Thomas's letters to Bottomley: (1) Letter 166, dated 16 Apr. 1916: 'I am sending a set of 4 I did lately, not because I think you will want to use them but because they are rather different in kind.' (2) Letter 167, dated 24 Apr. 1916: 'The household poems ought perhaps to appear as a bunch.'

The poems were not selected by Bottomley for inclusion in *AANP* but I assume Thomas used the typescript sent to Bottomley (or a copy of it) for his own selection for *EE*.

## 106 [1 *Bronwen*]

Bronwen was born on 29 Oct. 1902 and died on 29 Mar. 1975. Originally trained as a dress designer, she frequently acted as companion to older friends of her parents. Her first two husbands died tragically—one after an illness subsequent to a motor cycle accident, the other of a brain tumour. In between marriages and long illnesses she lived with her mother in Hampstead or Sheldon. While her third husband was in the R.A.F. during the last war she was a matron at Charterhouse. Subsequently, she and her husband retired to Eastbury where she spent her last years. She is survived by one son and three grandchildren.

See *TLFY*, pp. 193-4, which explains Thomas's love of the Essex place-names used in his poem. Thomas used local Ordnance Survey maps as a map-reading instructor at Hare Hall Camp.

## 107 [2 *Merfyn*]

Merfyn was born on 15 Jan. 1900 and died on 2 Aug. 1965, six months after his retirement as technical editor (from 1946 to 1965) of the journals *Bus and Coach* (and *Motor Transport*) which he joined in 1923 after qualifying as a draughtsman with A.E.C. and London General Omnibus Co. A founder member of the Institute of Road Transport Engineers. Served in England with a Kent Rifle Regiment in 1918; commissioned in 1940, he was evacuated from Calais and served with R.E.M.E. Corps in the Middle East 1941-6, attaining the rank of Major. A highly esteemed technical journalist whose articles were published in many countries. He is survived by his widow, one son, and two grandchildren.

*14-17* Thomas's children have recalled for me his informal lessons in natural history interlarded with fanciful tales of proverbs, folk stories, and songs of all kinds. As his letters to Frost show, Thomas was unhappily disappointed about Merfyn's adolescent interests, so unlike his own. Here are extracts from an unpublished memoir of his father recorded by Merfyn in 1952 for Rowland Watson:

> I did not understand him nor he me, and while I did not appreciate his point of view he could not or he would not see mine.... I have the most happy memories of our life together, of his gentle kindness, of his knowledge and appreciation of the countryside and the simple things of life which he instilled into me and which I retain today.... There were happy days walking across country when I learnt from him about trees and flowers and about birds and animals.

Some of Thomas's tales about proverbs appeared in *Four-and-Twenty Black-birds* (1915).

## 108 [3 *Myfanwy*]

Myfanwy, born on 16 Aug. 1910, was educated in Sevenoaks and Tonbridge during her mother's long illness and spent the weekdays with her aunt. Trained as a secretary, she held various posts with her uncle, with the B.B.C., with Henry Williamson, with Batsford's the publishers, and at Malvern College, before qualifying as a teacher. She settled with her mother at Eastbury and taught at a local school from 1954 to 1975. At one time sub-editor of the *Adelphi* magazine and a reviewer of children's books for *The Listener*, she organized the fund for the Memorial Window at Eastbury where she still lives and is the literary executrix of her parents' estates. She has one daughter and four grandchildren.

Thomas's letters to Robert Frost at this time contain many references to his financial situation and his plans to improve it by joining Frost in New Hampshire if the war were to end in 1916. The poet's determination to give all his children a country upbringing is best seen in his comments on 'Nature-teaching in schools' in *The South Country* (1909), pp. 141-6. The following extract concludes his argument (pp. 145-6):

> Yet Nature-study is not designed to produce naturalists, any more than music is taught in order to make musicians. If you produce nothing but naturalists you fail, and you will produce very few. The aim of study is to widen the culture of child and man, to do systematically what Mark Pattison tells us in his dry way he did for himself, by walking and outdoor sports, then—at the late age of seventeen—by collecting and reading such books as *The Natural History of Selborne*, and finally by a slow process of transition from natural history into 'the more abstract poetic emotion ... a conscious and declared poetical

sentiment and a devoted reading of the poets.' Geology did not come for another ten years, 'to complete the cycle of thought, and to give that intellectual foundation which is required to make the testimony of the eye, roaming over an undulating surface, fruitful and satisfying. When I came in after years to read *The Prelude* I recognized, as if it were my own history which was being told, the steps by which the love of the country boy for his hills and moors grew into poetical susceptibility for all imaginative presentations of beauty in every direction.' The botany, etc., would naturally be related to the neighbourhood of school or home; for there is no parish or district of which it might not be said, as Jefferies and Thoreau each said of his own, that it is a microcosm. By this means the natural history may easily be linked to a preliminary study of hill and valley and stream, the positions of houses, mills and villages, and the reasons for them, and the food supply, and so on, and this in turn leads on to—nay, involves—all that is most real in geography and history. The landscape retains the most permanent marks of the past, and a wise examination of it should evoke the beginnings of the majestic sentiment of our oneness with the future and the past, just as natural history should help to give the child a sense of oneness with all forms of life. To put it at its lowest, some such cycle of knowledge is needed if a generation that insists more and more on living in the country, or spending many weeks there, is not to be bored or to be compelled to entrench itself behind the imported amusements of the town.

## 109 [4 *Helen*]

Helen, born on 11 July 1877, died on 12 Apr. 1967. She lived at Forge House, Otford, Kent, after Edward's death, suffering increasingly for many years from delayed shock and nervous exhaustion, despite the conflicting remedies of various specialists. On their advice she returned intermittently to live in London and, in 1926, settled at 5, The Gables, Hampstead which was her principal home until March 1939. *As It Was*, a desperate attempt at psychotherapy, was begun at Otford and, like its sequel *World Without End*, completed in Hampstead. From about 1932 she spent more and more time at Starwell Farm, Sheldon, Chippenham, and finally settled there until 1954 when she joined her youngest daughter at Bridge Cottage, Eastbury, Berkshire. Despite failing eyesight she remained an active broadcaster, gardener, and countrywoman until her very last year. A memorial window to Edward and Helen Thomas, executed by Laurence Whistler and supported by public subscription, was dedicated in Eastbury Church on 16 Oct. 1971.

For some amplification of this intimate poem to his wife, see 'Edward Thomas: A Memorial Tribute' in *English*, vol. xxi, No. 109, pp. 18-21.

## 112 *When we two walked*

1 A reference to a long walk taken by the poet and his wife before Easter 1914.

## 115 [*I never saw that land before*]

For a discussion of the place of an imaginary land in Thomas's writings see *Edward Thomas (Writers of Wales)*, pp. 67-74.

## 119 *The sun used to shine*

The occasion of this poem—recalling the holiday spent by Thomas and his family with Frost's family in Herefordshire during August 1914—was probably the receipt of a letter from Frost on 21 May 1916 after a long silence. (Thomas's previous letter to Frost is dated 16 Mar. 1916 and was in answer to the letter that had arrived on his birthday, 3 Mar.)

## 121 *As the team's head brass*

This poem reflects the poet's maturing decision to abandon his job as a map-reading instructor and to apply for a commission with the possibility of a posting to France. His chief concern was the financial plight of his family. He was hoping for a Civil List Pension to relieve family needs and in June 1916 he was granted a £300 lump sum instead. See especially the following letters:

(1) to Eleanor Farjeon, 28 May 1916:

> We are only free in the evenings nowadays. They won't let us alone. We have to do the usual duties. Every N.C.O. is to be made universally competent. No doubt it is very good for us as well as for the country and I really am determined not to mind much. The new hours [i.e. the introduction of British Summer Time] give us a longer evening, so that we can still walk a little. I have even written several things which I send you.

(2) to Robert Frost, 10 June 1916:

> Now the Government instead of a pension is going to give me £300 in a lump. This will simplify some things. Mervyn's case, for example, especially as my engineer brother [Theodore] has promised to get him into a big motor works on September 1st and this is being settled. Also I am rather expecting I may get a commission before very long as an officer in the Anti-Aircraft Corps . . . I am accumulating such a mass of verse and I have an affection for so many.

(3) to Frost, 28 July 1916:

> A new step I have taken makes a good moment for writing. I offered myself for Artillery and today I was accepted, which means I shall go very soon to an Artillery School and be out in France or who knows where in a few months. After months of panic and uncertainty I feel much happier again except that I don't take easily to the trigonometry needed for artillery calculations. I have done very nearly all that I could do here in the way of teaching, lecturing, and taking charge of men in and out of doors. My old acquaintances were mostly moving out. The speeding up of things left no chance of enjoying the walks we used to have. So I had to go . . . Of course I can't write any more verses just now and have not done for a month or so. The last I did were during a 3 days' walk that Helen and I took at the end of June when I had a few days leave due to me. We had fine bright weather and saw [Vivian Locke] Ellis and a few others in Sussex and Kent. It was too short. I can only be content now in regular almost continuous work when I have no time for comparisons.

## 124 [*Song 3*]

The composition of this poem—a reflection of the poet's lifelong interest in folk-songs (see his *The Pocket Book of Poems and Songs for the Open Air* (1907))—caused him a great deal of trouble, as his letters to Eleanor Farjeon of 19 and 24 June 1916 (*TLFY*, pp. 199-200), and the three manuscript drafts in $M_2$, show. Behind the poem, too—especially the reference to burning his letters in line 6—was the upheaval caused by the loss of his hill-top study and the final move from Steep to Essex (see *GB*, Letter 169).

## 127 [*There was a time*]

This poem was composed during 'three days sick and confined to the camp, practically to the hut and this [i.e. Poems 125-7] is the result' (*TLFY*, p. 200). For the poet's attitude to the poem—which reflects his decision to apply for a commission—see a letter to Eleanor Farjeon dated 29 June 1916: 'I wish you could shut your eyes to many big things as I do without trying. If they do prey on me I don't know it. But then I wasn't in a bad mood when I wrote those lines you thought sick—I think you meant the longest of those three. I thought it was more than a shade heroic.'

## 128 *The Green Roads*

See Thomas's letter to Eleanor Farjeon, 29 June 1916 (*TLFY*, p. 202): 'This is the latest. A wet warm free afternoon. The forest is a fragment left 6 miles from here [Gidea Park, Romford, Essex], the best of all this county. I go there every time I can. There is a cottage not far off where you might like to stay some day. The people have been there 53 years. You can't imagine a wilder quieter place.'

## 129 *When first*

*13 The twelfth*: although Thomas did not move to Berryfield Cottage, Ashford (near Steep), until November 1906, he and Helen had been looking for a house there, near Bedales School, the previous year. Parts of his *The Heart of England* (1906), written in 1905, suggest a knowledge of this district.

## 130 *The Gallows*

Selsfield House, East Grinstead was the home of Vivian Locke Ellis where Thomas had spent some time as a paying guest in the winter of 1912 and in the early spring of 1914. He and Helen spent the last four days of his week's leave (30 June–6 July 1916) at Selsfield visiting friends, including Harry Hooton (in Coulsden) and Eleanor Farjeon (in London).

In spite of its grim undertones of front line warfare, this poem illustrates Thomas's close involvement with his children during his many Army leaves. See especially a letter to Eleanor Farjeon dated 7 July 1916 (*TLFY*, p. 202): 'At Ellises I could not help writing these four verses on the theme of some stories I used to tell Baba [Myfanwy] there. The other 3 [the three verses of 'The Dark Forest' (Poem 131)] I believe are no good, the forest is perhaps a too obvious metaphor.' A recently found *Helen* manuscript is headed 'For Baba'.

## 131 [*The Dark Forest*]

A final stanza—the last entry in $M_2$—probably reflects the poet's feelings after the London visit to his parents. Soon afterwards his mother had an eye operation. See *GB*, Letter 172, dated 2 Oct. 1916: 'my Mother in London. I must see as often as possible . . . She is very lonely with us all away. Not that she complains.' See too the note to Poem 130. By removing this final personal stanza Thomas makes the 'metaphor' of the forest less obvious:

>               beloved and lover or child and
> Not even ‸ ~~mother and child or sister and brother~~,
> One from within, one from
> Without the forest could recognize each other,
> Since they have changed their home.

## 132 *When he should laugh*

See Thomas's letter to Robert Frost, dated 28 July 1916, announcing his decision to accept a commission in the Artillery: 'No news. My Mother has lately been operated on for cataract and is in a nursing home waiting to see again. She is not happy over my new chance of going out as an officer—I ought to be an officer in less than a few months. Nor is Helen. She is not often happy now. She is tired and anxious.'

## 133 *The Swifts*

See three letters to Eleanor Farjeon:

(1) (Postmark) 11 Aug. 1916, 'Hospital—Thursday': 'I entered this place on Tuesday morning [with a swollen arm after vaccination] and ever since have been too bored to do anything but wish myself out. I can't read. This afternoon I had to write something. I wrote these 2 verses, which I am afraid may simply make you think them perfectly true.'

(2) From Steep, 20 Aug. 1916: 'Don't you worry about typing those 2 verses, in which I have changed "August blue" to "harvest blue". I was glad to have them to write anyway—shall be lucky to do more till the swifts are back again.'

(3) From R.A. School, Handel Street, W.C.3 (*TLFY*, p. 213): 'By the way, you misread the poem you didn't so much like—about the swifts—missing the point that year after year I see them, *realising it is the last time*, i.e. just before they go away for the winter (early in August). Perhaps it is too much natural history.' This last point echoes the letter to his aunt about a re-telling of the Mabinogian stories (14 Feb. 1915): 'As they stand the old stories are works of art in which, as in every work of art, the writer accepts many things he could not explain and feels no need of explanation. If he did feel that need he would make a work of philosophy or natural history, and not a work of art.'

See also *Berg FNB* 80, undated, after 2 June 1915, between entries for Poems 80 and 82: 'Swift with tail and wings so sharp and ? It seems the bow has flown off with the arrow.'

## 134  *Blenheim Oranges*

See letters to Eleanor Farjeon:

(1) dated 27 Aug. 1916: 'I have been resting yesterday and today at Rusham Road. We get practically every weekend. The result is I got tired of logarithms and wrote 8 verses which you see before you. When I come I should like to borrow about the last 12 things I have written. I want to send them to the prospective publisher I told you about [Roger Ingpen], with these if they are good enough.'

(2) Dated 19 Sept. 1916: 'In case I don't [see you] could you send me a copy of those last verses—the Blenheim Oranges—of mine? I can't find one or the original. You will see I have written some more too—if you *can* see the faint type. Perhaps one of them is better than the others.'

*17–24* These lines recall Thomas's early and continued affection for the old London houses of his youth which play such a significant part in his novel *The Happy-Go-Lucky Morgans* (1913). (Cf. E. M. Forster's description of one such local house, 'Battersea Rise' in his *Abinger Harvest* (Part III—'The Past').) See *GB*, Letter 66, dated 27 Mar. 1907:

> Then I do want to arrange my chiefly pathetic memories of the Suburbs—their grave charming old Annes now tumbling down at the feet of the villa-builders—their little bits of waste ground—my own special memories—a little girl, the first whose sex I dimly knew (when I was 7 or 8)—the quite new houses so difficult to like and yet to be liked. But of course not 100 people want such a book.

## 135  [*That girl's clear eyes*] [*Sonnet* 6]

There is no hard evidence to explain this poem, which seems like a response to a portrait in the Royal Artillery School, Handel St., where the poet was studying as an Officer Cadet. If so, 'Seventeen Thirty-Nine' (l. 14) is the date of the painting. But the poem may be an echo of a minor eighteenth-century poem unidentifiable. See letter to Frost on 11 Sept. 1916 about Frost's suggestion that he and Thomas should collaborate on an anthology of love poems, 'The Old Cloak', perhaps suggested by Thomas's 'Words' (Poem 77):

> I don't believe I can do much yet at 'The Old Cloak'. You can't imagine the degree of my disinclination for books. Sometimes I say I will read Shakespeare's sonnets again and I do, or half do, but never more than that. I should love to do it with you. I thought of what love poems could go in—could Burns's 'Whistle and I'll come to ye, my lad'? There are the songs in the very earliest Elizabethan dramatists. There's a deal of Chaucer, Shakespeare, Cowper, Wordsworth and the ballads: some Crabbe: one poem apiece out of Prior and several minor 18th century people: a few of Blake's. But I don't begin to look at books: I must keep all my *conscious attention* for my work.

## 136 [*What will they do?*]

The initial note of regret with which the poem begins presumably reflects the poet's last visit to Steep before he moved his family to High Beech, near Loughton, Essex. His cottage in Steep village was already let to the poet John Freeman, with whom Thomas's younger daughter was staying: his elder daughter was living with her aunt in London; his son, now an engineering apprentice, was lodging in Walthamstow. Helen was on a walking tour of the Lake District with her sister Irene—who had recently lost her husband after a long illness—and Thomas was left to arrange the final move from Steep, which he visited once more during his final training at Codford.

## 137 *The Trumpet*

Thomas was eager to begin his field training as an officer-cadet, after the (for him) exacting mathematical training at Handel St., London. He was now an experienced N.C.O. with considerable knowledge of camp life. The trumpeters at the Trowbridge Barracks attracted his attention from the first. See two letters to Eleanor Farjeon:

(1) 24 Sept. 1916: 'We are in tents and so we see the night sky. The trumpet blows for everything and I like that too, though the trumpeter is not excellent. We have had our costume criticised a good deal and have had to buy gloves and so on. But it is not so bad as it was painted . . . I hope you liked some of the verses.'

(2) Wednesday, n.d. (Eleanor Farjeon has the sequence of letters wrong here, I believe. She thinks 'The Trumpet' belongs to November. See *TLFY*, p. 218): 'However you can see I have some ease, because I have written some verses suggested by the trumpet calls which go all day. They are not well done and the trumpet is cracked, but the Reveille pleases me (more than it does most sleepers). Here is the result. You see I have written it with only capitals to mark lines, because people are all around me and I don't want them to know.'

### 138 [*The Child in the Orchard*]

Some background to this poem is expanded in the poet's letters:

(1) To Eleanor Farjeon on 2 Nov. 1916: 'also to send you some verses I managed to write before the end of my leave'.

(2) On 6 Nov. 1916: 'Thank you for typing the verses. I see that "At the age of six" [l. 20] is a rather rough way of explaining who speaks. But he did tell me he was six too and seemed to realise he had a long way to go.'

(3) To Robert Frost from Trowbridge, on 4 Nov. 1916: 'One day when the sun was warm we bathed in the Frome. This is the country I came to when I wrote my "Swinburne" [May–June 1912]. It has two good little rivers, one in a shallow level valley, the other in a steepsided narrow one. There is a castle and many fine old houses near, and Salisbury Plain just too far off for our short afternoons, but its old White Horse plainly visible all day.'

(4) To Frost, during a week-end leave at High Beech, near Loughton, Essex, on 19 Oct. 1916: 'I have just written the second thing since I left London a month ago. If I can type the two you shall see them. I am wondering if any of these last few sets of verses have pleased you at all.'

### 139 *Lights Out*

For the use of the 'forest as metaphor', see Notes to Poems 130 and 131 above.
    Two letters to Eleanor Farjeon are relevant:

(1) From Trowbridge on 6 Nov. 1916: 'Now I have actually done still another piece which I call "Lights Out". It sums up what I have often thought at that call. I wish it were as brief—2 pairs of long notes. I wonder is it nearly as good as it might be.'

(2) On 11 Nov. 1916: 'Oh, Granville Barker is in my room now, but is just being shunted off to a School for Coast Defence. I suppose his friends have urged his country not to risk his life. I hope I shall always be as eager to risk mine as I have been these last few months.'

### 140 *The long small room*

In his letter to Eleanor Farjeon of 13 Nov. Thomas writes: 'I am worried about the impression the willow made on you. As a matter of fact I started with the last line as what I was working to. I am only fearing it has a sort of Japanesy suddenness of ending. But it is true, whether or not it is a legitimate switch to make. I will think of it as much like somebody else as possible.' (For this reference to Japanese verse see Thomas's interest in the work of Yone Noguchi in *GB*, and, more particularly, his *Lafcadio Hearn*, pp. 71–82.)

## 141  *The Sheiling*

Gordon Bottomley—Thomas's friend and correspondent over thirteen years—lived at The Sheiling, Silverdale, near Carnforth. Thomas spent three days from his long post-OCTU leave to visit Bottomley. The poem is a crystallization of their friendship and recalls the attraction of Bottomley's cultured, restful invalid existence for Thomas. (See the introduction to *GB*, pp. 2-7, C. C. Abbott's *Gordon Bottomley, Poems and Plays* (1953), and *Poet and Painter: Being the correspondence between G. B. and Paul Nash 1940-1946*, ed. C. C. Abbott and Anthony Bertram (1953).)

In some ways this poem is a late reply to Bottomley's poem to Thomas which precedes Bottomley's *Riding to Lithend* (1907). Both poets were interested in Old Icelandic literature and, because Thomas's comment on the 'Japanesy ending' to 'The long small room' (Poem 140) suggests a mood of retrospective survey at this time, it is not over-fanciful to detect an echo of scaldic alliteration and assonance—as available then in English translations—in some of these stanzas.

*11* In the *Bod* manuscript Thomas alters 'Soft' to 'Safe', possibly in deference to Bottomley's ill health and inability to take up any form of national service.

*16 maker*: a pun on the Scottish word for poet, as well as a tribute to Emily Bottomley's gifts as a home-maker.

## 142  [*The Lane*]

This poem is written on a loose leaf inserted into the book in which *Bod* is written. At the bottom of the leaf is a note by Helen Thomas: 'Sent from Codford', where Thomas was awaiting embarkation. In a letter to Helen from Codford, dated 22 Jan. 1917, he wrote: 'You never mentioned receiving those verses about Green Lane, Froxfield [near Steep]. Did you get them? They were written in December and suggested by our last walk there in September.' Perhaps these are the verses referred to in his letter to Eleanor Farjeon from Trowbridge on 2 Nov. 1916: 'I did something else too coming down in the train on a long dark journey when people were talking and I wasn't, but I have got it still to finish.' If the poem was written in two stages, this may explain the discontinuity suggested by the dots after l. 8.

## 143  [*Out in the dark*]

Thomas liked his new home at High Beech. See:

(1) His letter to Elinor Frost on 27 Nov. 1917: 'Except on Saturdays and Sundays and holidays we see nothing only aeroplanes and deer in the forest. Baba [Myfanwy] has no companions. She goes about telling herself stories . . . The forest is beautiful, oaks, hornbeams, beeches, bracken, hollies, and some heather. But it is really High Beach, not Beech, on account of the pebbly soil. There are 7 or 8 miles of forest, by 1 or 2 miles wide, all in the high ground, with many tiny ponds and long wide glades.'

(2) A letter to Eleanor Farjeon from R.A. Mess, Tin Town, Lydd, on 27 Dec. 1916: 'I am going to send you in exchange some verses I made on Sunday. It is really Baba who speaks, not I. Something she felt put me on to it. But I am afraid I am meddling now. A real poem would include and imply all these things I am writing, or so I fancy. . . . It is curious how I feel no anxiety or trouble as soon as I am back here, though I was so very glad to be at home.'

(3) A letter to Robert Frost (headed 'High Beech' but sent from Lydd) on 31 Dec. 1916:

> I was home for Christmas by an unexpected piece of luck. We were very happy with house-work and wood gathering in the forest and a few walks. We had some snow and sunshine on Christmas day. Mervyn's holiday coincided with mine. Some of the time I spent at my Mother's house and in London buying the remainder of my things for the front. . . . I wonder have you had your duplicate of the Ms. which I sent over a month ago? It looks now as if I should not see the proofs [of *EE*]. Bottomley or John Freeman will do it for me. . . . When I am alone—as I am during the evening just now because the officer who shares my room is away—I hardly know what to do. I can't write now and still less can I read. I have rhymed but I have burnt my rhymes and feel proud of it.

## 144 *Last Poem*

This poem is on the last page of the diary kept by Thomas during his last three months as a soldier. The diary was in the possession of his son, Merfyn, until his death in 1965, and was rediscovered by Merfyn's son (Edward) in the summer of 1970. It was first printed along with the diary and a foreword in *The Anglo-Welsh Review* (Autumn, 1971); the diary is now reprinted here as an Appendix, pp.173 – 94. The poem was written on 13 Jan. 1917, at Lydd, two days after the poet's last leave when he said good-bye to his family. See diary entry for 11 Jan. and especially the entry for 13 Jan. 1917: 'Cold drizzle. Horton [his C.O.] and the battery left early for Codford. Even wrote verses. Early to bed.' There is an identical copy of the first five lines in Helen's hand dated 13 Feb. 1917.

# APPENDIX

# DIARY OF EDWARD THOMAS
## *1 January–8 April 1917*

THE private diary kept by Edward Thomas during his last three months as a soldier is here printed for the third time. It is written in a small (3 in. × 5¾ in.) Walker's Back-Loop pocket-book, bound in pigskin and priced at two shillings; the cover and pages are curiously creased, which suggests that he was carrying the diary either on 8 April, when he was knocked over by the blast from a 5·9 shell, or on the morning of 9 April, when he was killed at an Observation Post while directing the fire of 244 Battery during the opening barrage of the Battle of Arras. The diary was given to his son, Merfyn, who died in 1965, and it was re-discovered in 1970 by *his* son, Edward, among various documents and papers that had been deposited for safety while the poet's grandson was abroad. The diary is here printed with the kind permission of the poet's daughter, Myfanwy, and of his grandson, Edward, who owns it. I do not think that the previous biographers of Edward Thomas have seen this diary, although many of the facts and laconic observations of the notebook are sometimes expanded and differently angled in the poet's letters to his family and friends, especially in letters to his wife Helen, to his brother Julian, and to such close friends as Robert Frost, Gordon Bottomley, and Eleanor Farjeon.

The diary is written in cramped handwriting with numerous abbreviations.[1] It is not easy to read with the naked eye and in places the heavy creasing and thin ink make it almost indecipherable. In the present version—which is based on a careful transcription made first by the poet's grandson, then checked by his two daughters, and finally prepared by me from a magnified copy of the original—all abbreviations have been silently expanded. I have also retained the diary's spelling of French names and the poet's spelling of 'Bosh'.

Perhaps the most interesting single item in the notebook is the poem written on the last page and dated '13.i.17'; undoubtedly this is the last poem that Edward Thomas wrote. A fair copy of ll. 1–5 was made by Helen Thomas; the poem was not published until 1971. As far as one can tell from the poet's correspondence, this is only a draft version. In the various notebooks that contain his poems—both those in private hands and those available in various public libraries in England and America—there is sufficient evidence to state that it is very rare to find that a first draft of any of his poems remained unaltered in the final version. The poem shows the strong influence of Shakespeare's sonnets, for, as the diary and the letters show, he read Shakespeare regularly each night during these last months of his life.

To my mind, the diary itself offers a more compelling interest than the new poem: like his own anthology, *This England*, it is as full of his character 'as an egg is of meat' and seems to contain the germs of ideas, books, and poems that were never to be written but that were surely present in his mind. Even more clearly it reveals the consistency of the poet's entire writing life, grounded as that was upon his powerful sensuous response to the world of

---

[1] Four pages of the diary are reproduced in *The Anglo-Welsh Review*, Autumn 1971, pp. 9–11. The diary is carefully phrased and Thomas corrects words and phrases as in all his working drafts. The twenty cancelled readings in the diary are not shown in the present text.

living and natural things. At the same time we are made aware of the self-contained, efficient officer who astonished his literary friends, who mostly seem to recall in their memoirs the self-doubting and despondent literary 'failure' that they had assumed Edward Thomas to be during the two years before the war. Apart from the various tributes sent to Helen in letters from his fellow soldiers, the best portrait of 2/Lt. P. E. Thomas was given in 1930 by his commanding Officer (Major Franklin Lushington) in Chapter Five of *The Gambardier* by 'Mark Severn':

'Among the subalterns T. Tyler [i.e. Thomas] alone was reliable and helpful. He was old enough to be Shadbolt's [i.e. Lushington's] father and before the war had achieved a name for himself as a writer . . . He carried on quietly and patiently until he was killed about two months later. His serene and kindly presence and quiet dry humour did much to alleviate the squalid miseries of life for his companions.'

True to lifelong habit, Edward Thomas kept his own moments of self-doubt and distrust to himself. The inner mood of his life in the front line is conveyed more unequivocally in his letters to Robert Frost, to whom, at this time, he seemed ever ready to open some of the otherwise unspoken thoughts of head and heart. Here are three significant extracts from his unpublished letters:

(1) 6 March 1917. 'I have time to spare but I can't talk. You don't answer, and I am inhibiting introspection except when I wake up and hear the shelling and wonder whether I ought to move my bed away from the window to the inner side where there is more masonry—more to resist and more to fall on me. But it is no use thinking like this' . . . So far it excites but doesn't disturb, or at any rate doesn't upset or unfit.

'I hear my book is coming out soon. Did the duplicate verses[2] ever reach you? You never said so. But don't think I mind. I should like to be a poet, just as I should like to live, but I know as much about my chances in either case, and I don't really trouble about either. Only I want to come back more or less complete.'

(2) 8 March 1917. 'Yesterday was cold and raw and I had to be indoors except for one hour and I became very depressed and solitary by the evening. Very soon, I expect to have no time or room left for depression.'

'I know some things about houses now that you don't know. The houses I observe from, for example, are still modern small houses, the last left standing before you come to the first line trenches. . . . No Man's Land is 150 yards wide. These modern houses have all been hit and downstairs is a mixture of bricks, mortar, bedsteads and filth. Upstairs you spy out through tiles at the enemy, who knows perfectly well you are there in one of the houses and some day will batter them all down. . . . You can't paint death living in them.—As I went to the village house today I heard a very young child talking in another equally exposed house in the same street. Someone too poor or too helpless or what to leave even these places. But I positively am not going to describe any more except for a living.'

---

[2] A duplicate set of the typescripts of *Poems by Edward Eastaway*, Thomas's first volume of poetry, published by Selwyn & Blount. Frost never received this set: at least I have been unable to trace them among his papers, and I assume they were lost at sea.

(3) 2 April 1917. 'Otherwise I have done all the things so far asked of me without making any mess and I have mingled satisfaction with dis-satisfaction in about the usual proportion, comfort and discomfort . . . I think I get surer of some primitive things that one has to get sure of, about myself and other people, and I think this is not due simply to being older. In short, I am glad I came out and I think less about return than I thought I should—partly no doubt I inhibit the idea of return. I only think by flashes of the things at home that I used to enjoy and should again. I enjoy many of them out here when the sun shines and at early morning and late afternoon. I doubt if anybody here thinks less of home than I do and yet I doubt if anybody loves it more.'

These letters to Frost provide a significant counterbass to the rather jerky melody of the diary. Taken together they confirm the opinion of his fellows about his steadying influence on this raw battery of young men under fire for the first time. Surprisingly, too, for one who began his career with so much shyness even at giving map-reading instruction, Thomas emerges from the diary as a good soldier with a sharp eye and quiet courage to meet the essentials of military duty. Again, the diary and the letters underline the poet's capacity for silent enjoyment of—is 'communion with' too strong a phrase?—the seen world of nature. The numerous jottings about the weather, the record of birds and plants, the direct response to the ruin of human dwellings—all these are not the random notes of an escapist. He was undoubtedly making a raw record on which to base his letters home, but, in another sense, he was writing for dear life. Had he survived, the diary would have provided the material for another imaginative work, unlike anything he had written before and certainly not a book that 'merely described for a living'. For this last diary continues his lifelong habit of observing accurately and recording his response to the natural world. His first book, *Woodland Life*, contained such a record of the natural world from 1 April 1895 to 30 March 1896, and many of his travelling records—often written in pencil in notebooks exactly like this diary—have survived from the twenty years of his writing life. His various topographical works were based on such records and his poetry, too, returns frequently to moods, incidents, scenes, and memories that date back almost twenty years before the first nature poem was composed in November 1914.

Elsewhere[3] I have argued that to understand the intense significance of these timeless, but accurately recalled, moments of communion with the natural world is necessary before one can understand the peculiar quality of 'sincerity' that is the hallmark of Thomas's poetry. This diary, I hope, helps to confirm this view and substantiates the remark to Frost that 'I think I get surer of some primitive things that one has got to get sure of, about myself and other people'. I find the diary most moving because of its subdued tone. Through his gifted eye and sure pen one can catch a glimpse both of the fearful tragedy of the 'Great War' and the low-keyed heroic strength of one poet's inner certitude.

1917
JANUARY

1. Shooting with 15 pounders and then 6″ howitzers. All week at Lydd, I being f/c [fire control officer] or observer daily, with map work for next

---

[3] *Edward Thomas* (*Writers of Wales*), ch. III, pp. 36–66.

day at night. Thorburn away. Beautiful clear bright weather always, but sometimes cold.

5. Left Lydd on mobilisation leave. Night at Rusham Road with Father and Mother.

6. Julian to breakfast. With Mother to stores. Lunch with Eleanor and tea with Joan and Bertie [Farjeon]. Home with Bronwen (returning from Chiswick). All well.

7. Walks with Helen and children. Fine day.

8. Eleanor came and stayed night. Wrote cheques for next 6 months.

9. Eleanor left. Helen and I walked in forest.

10. Dentist's. Lunch with Jones and Harry [Hooton]. Tea with Ivy Ransome and then Ingpen and Davies. Saw V. H. Collins. Home.

11. Said goodbye to Helen, Mervyn and Baba. Bronwen to Rusham Road. Lunched with Mrs. Freeman: afterwards saw [E. S. P.] Haynes and McCabe. Tea with Jesse [Berridge] and T. Clayton and met Lipchitz. Supper at Rusham Road with all my brothers.

12. A letter from Helen. Goodbye to Bronwen, Mother and Father. Lunch with Mary [Valon, Helen's sister] and Margaret [Mary Valon's daughter]. Saw Irene [MacArthur]. To Lydd and found only Horton[4] and Grier; Thorburn gone on to Codford. Letters from Helen and [G. R.] Blanco White; to Helen, Mother, Mrs. de la Mare, Frost, [Vivian Locke] Ellis, [C.] Hodson, Eleanor, and John Freeman.

13. Nothing to do but test compass which never gives same results. Walk and tea with Flawn. Cold drizzle. Horton and the battery left early for Codford. Even wrote verses.[5] Early to bed.

14. A Sunday and no letters as I am supposed to be at Codford. Letters to Helen and Blanco White. A bright cold day. Walked with Flawn through Old Romney and Ivychurch. Flawn to tea with me. Packing.

15. Up 6. Packing. Left Lydd at 9 with Q.M.S. [Quartermaster Sergeant] and Grier and 3 men. Light snow and red sun. 4 hours to spare in London but could only see T. Clayton and D. [A. Duncan] Williams: could not find J. Freeman. Then to Codford in the dark, writing to Helen and beginning 'A Sentimental Journey'. Arrived too late for dinner.

---

[4] A fellow officer. Others mentioned in the Diary are Berrington, Cassells, Fenner, Flawn, Lushington, Rubin, Smith, Thorburn, and Witchall.

[5] See Poem 144.

16. Letters from Helen, Eleanor, Mervyn, [Edward] Garnett, [John W.] Haines, Mrs. Ellis. Took route march to Wigtye, Stockton, Sherrington, and had great luck in short cuts and byeroads over river. A frosty clear day: men singing 'Dixie', 'There's a long long trail of winding [*sic*] to the land of my dreams', and 'We're here because we're here' to the tune of Auld Lang Syne. Only Smith and I and Capt. Fenner left of the 6 officers. Afternoon walked with Smith to Chitterne and had tea there. Evening dined together and talked about practical education—pronunciation of 'girl', 'soot' and 'historian'—and about rhymes to eye.

17. Light snow in night; hard frost. Men on fatigues or drawing overseas clothes etc. Office full of boots, blankets, pails, axes, shovels, dixies, stretchers etc. Route march to Tytherington, Heytesbury and Knook. Afternoon walked over Downs by Stockton Wood to Chilmark with Smith: tea at the inn and Smith played ragtime etc. A cloudy clear frosty day. Back over the downs on a dark night, but only went astray 200 yards. Letter from Helen, Mother and John Freeman. Letters to Helen, Mother, Haines, Eleanor.

18. Letters from Helen, Hodson, Mrs. de la Mare, Father. Letters to Helen, Irene, Father. To Warminster to the bank. Still frosty. Afternoon lectured on map-reading. Orderly officer for camp from 6 p.m. Indoors all evening, talking to Smith about marching songs etc.

19. Letters from Mother, Helen, Miss Coltman, [W. H.] Hudson. Letters to Mother, Helen, M. Freeman, Lady Newbolt, Oscar [Thomas, Edward's fourth brother]. Morning orderly officer—latrines etc.—lectured on maps—paid Battery. Afternoon learnt to ride motor cycle. Mild and drizzly. Guns are due to arrive. A cake from Mother. Shakespeare's Sonnets from Helen. Capt. Fenner talks of having to take sick leave.

20. Letter from J. Freeman. Letters to Garnett, [James] Guthrie, Harry, Coltman. Mild snowy. Arranging stores. Guns arriving. Smith to Bath. So I had to see to unloading and parking the guns till dark. No use walking after dark. The roads are pitch dark and crowded with men going to cinemas, darkness worse from blaze of motor lamps and electric light in camps nearby. Long queues waiting outside cinema at 5.30. Tested battery compass. Talk with Fenner about martens in Ireland, badgers, plovers, barrows etc.

21. No church parade for me. 9.30-1.30 walked over Stockton Down, the Bake, and under Grovely Wood to Barford St. Martin, Burcombe, and to lunch at Netherhampton House with Newbolts. Freezing drizzle—freezes on ground, white grass and icy roads. 2 families of vagrants in green road roasting a corpse of something by slow wood fire. Beautiful

Downs, with one or two isolated thatched barns, ivied ash trees, and derelict threshing machine. Old milestones lichened as with battered gold and silver nails. Back by train at 5. Tea alone. Guns in line out on parade square. Smith back. Letter from Helen, Ingpen, Eleanor, Hudson. Letter to Helen, Ingpen. Talk with Fenner after dinner about fishing—river and sea.

22. Set the men branding and sorting stores. Left at 10.30 for Gloster to see Haines. Still frosty and dull. Gloster at 2.50. Sat till 12.15 gossiping about Frost, de la Mare, and the army, marching songs etc. Haines gave me Frost's 'Mountain Interval'.

23. With Mrs. Haines and Robin most of morning. 3.30 left Gloster via Mangotsfield and Bath for Codford. Read 'Mountain Interval'. Horton, Rubin and Thorburn back. Fenner merry; he is probably to go on sick leave. He and Rubin returned late and had a noisy parting from 2 others. Thorburn had a screaming nightmare.

24. All men on fatigues. A short walk with Thorburn to test compasses. Letters from Helen, Father, Mother, Harry. Letters to Helen, Father, Mother, M. Freeman. Parcel of medicines etc. from Helen, cigars from Harry. Walked in afternoon with Thorburn to Chilmark for tea, and back over frosty Downs with new moon and all stars. But my ankles chafed by new boots lame me.

25. Resting my sore ankles. Dial sights tested and stores arranged for packing tomorrow. Guns leave on 27th and Battery on 29th. Fenner is to go to hospital and Horton to take charge. Very cold with East wind. Letters from Oscar, letters to Oscar, Helen, Mother, Mrs. de la Mare, Frost, John Freeman, Mrs. M. Freeman, Harry, Eleanor. Capt. Lushington is to be our new o/c [Officer Commanding 244 Battery (Acting Major Lushington)] and to take us out.

26. Letters from Helen, Eleanor, letters to Helen, Mervyn. Loading lorries and attaching guns to 4-wheel drives—standing out in dusty icy East wind doing nothing but getting cold and dirty. I sleep badly too. Also I have taken charge of mess and mess accounts. Thorburn is on my nerves—he had a nightmare lately—asking 'Can you tell me how much 55 lbs. is?'—the weight of officers' luggage. I feel useless. Am still in slacks and shoes on account of bad ankles. Thorburn and I dining alone, the others with Capt. Lushington in the village—our mess kit being packed. Can't even walk far enough to get warm. Thorburn goes tomorrow with guns. Dined with him and then talked about philosophy and poetry, and Yes and Perhaps, and the lyric and the Bible. I have a cold. The frost is worse tonight.

27. A clear windy frosty dawn, the sun like a bright coin between the knuckles of opposite hills seen from sidelong. A fox. A little office work. Telegram to say Baba was at Ransome's, so I walked over Downs by Chicklade Bottom and the Fonthills to Hatch, and blistered both feet badly. House full of ice and big fires. Sat up with Ivy till 12 and slept till 8. Another fine bright frosty day on the

28th. Wrote to Bronwen, Helen, Ivy, Eleanor. Letters from Bronwen, Helen, Mother, Eleanor. Slept late. Rested my feet, talking to the children or Ivy cooking with Kitty Gurd. Hired a bicycle to save walking. Such a beautiful ride after joining the Mere and Amesbury Road at Fonthill Bishop—hedgeless roads over long sloping downs with woods and sprinkled thorns, carved with old tracks which junipers line—an owl and many rabbits—a clear pale sky and but a faint sunset—a long twilight lasting till 6. We are to move at 6.30 a.m. tomorrow. Horton and Smith and I dined together laughing at imbecile jests and at Smith's own laughing. Had to change in order to send home my soiled things. Letters. Mess accounts and cheques to tradesmen.

29. Up at 5. Very cold. Off at 6.30, men marching in frosty dark to station singing 'Pack up your troubles in your old kitbag'. The rotten song in the still dark brought one tear. No food or tea—Freezing carriage. Southampton at 9.30 and there had to wait till dusk, walking up and down, watching ice-scattered water, gulls and dark wood beyond, or London Scottish playing improvised Rugger, or men dancing to concertina, in a great shed between railway and water. Smith and I got off for lunch after Horton and Capt. Lushington returned from theirs. Letter to Helen from 'South Western Hotel', where sea-captains were talking of the 'Black Adder' and of 'The Black Ball Line' that used to go to Australia. Hung about till dark—the seagulls as light failed nearly all floated instead of flying—then sailed at 7. Thorburn turned up. Now I'm in 2nd officer's cabin with Capt. and Horton, the men outside laughing and joking and saying fucking. Q.W.R.'s [Queen's Westmorland(?) Rifles] and Scottish and a Field Battery and 236 S.B. [Siege Battery], also on 'The Mona Queen'. Remember the entirely serious and decorous writing in urinal whitewash—name, address, unit, and date of sailing. A tumbling crossing, but rested.

30. Arrived Havre 4 a.m. Light of stars and windows of tall pale houses and electric arcs on quay. March through bales of cotton in sun to camp. The snow first emptying its castor of finest white. Tents. Mess full of subalterns censoring letters. Breakfast at 9.45 a.m. on arrival. Afternoon in Havre, which Thorburn likes because it is French. Mess unendurably

hot and stuffy, tent unendurably cold till I got into my blankets. Slept well in fug. Snow at night.

31. Had to shift our lines in snow. 12 to a tent with 2 blankets each. Ankles bad. Nearly all water frozen in taps and basins. Mess crowded—some standing. Censoring letters about the crossing and the children and ailments etc. at home. Had to make a speech explaining that men need not be shy about writing familiar letters home. At 'Nouvel Hotel', Havre, while we had tea, waitress kissing a Capt. and arranging for another visit. 4f. for 2 teas. Battery had to be specially warned against venereal in Havre. Read Sonnets in evening: to bed at 9 to escape hot stuff room. Officers coming and going. Some faces you just see, drinking once and never again. More fine snow like sago.

## FEBRUARY

1. Freezing and overcast. Hospital train goes through camp (wounded men say we have advanced at N. Chapelle). Battery on route march. I arrange to eat midday ration in tent to save lunch in Mess (2f.50). Guns and stores not here yet. Other officers mostly in Havre but my ankle prevents me. Down in lorry to Ordnance Store for field boots. Snow. Route march, but not for me. I write and censor letters. No fire in the mess till 3 p.m. Guns are coming today. Detachments reorganised.— Mess fills up.—Cockney rankers with two stars come in and drink standing and talk of Singapore and Pekin and duration officers look up. Some rapacious and sneering, some gentle. Read Sonnets.

2. A still colder night and my new boots hurt my ankles like the old. Tried to get shoes from Ordnance in vain—rode past quays and stores of hay, grain, cotton etc.—cattle—German prisoners—French sentries hooded with long loose cloaks and long rifles and curved bayonets. After-noon into Havre to look for low shoes—but all too tight: bought low soft boots. Tea in teashop with Thorburn. In a hole over value of English shillings. Bought a good root stick with leather sling for 2f.50. Hard clear night again. All other officers out. Argument with Thorburn about morals, shame, whether poets must go through not only 'sin' but 'repentance'— Dante, Shakespeare. Cold supper in our cold tent—iron ration and cheese and marmalade.

3. Not quite so cold. Overhauling guns and rearranging stores on road-side by camp. A pleasant change, but not very much for me to do. Shall the guns be George, Andrew, Patrick, David? Again on the guns in after-noon. 236 Battery leave tonight: most of the officers are in Havre ignorant. All 244 except Smith dined and wined at the Normandie for 10fr. The

view is that it could possibly be better placed. Back to Rest Camp 9.30—great stark ships black with level flecked snow below and big engines and troops arriving.

4. Cold and bright again. Took the section sliding, then work on guns. At 11 came warning to move at 5.30. Packing, Censoring. New servant—Taylor. Asked if he had done anything of the kind before, said 'I've a wife and family and I know what comforts are.' Started at 4.45 for station with guns—held up 1½ hours by train across road—2 hours at station doing nothing, 1½ hours entraining guns—platform all cotton bales and men singing 'The nightingales are singing in the pale moonlight'. ('There's a long long trail awinding'). Sgt. Major did practically all the work.— The long waiting before train starts—men quite silent after first comic cries of 'All tickets' and imitating cattle (35 men in each cattle truck: we have a compartment to 2 officers). As we start at 11 suddenly the silent men all yell 'Hurray' but are silent before we are clear of long desolate platform of cotton and trampled snow and electric light.

5. At 7 a.m. after many stops and starts we were close under partly wooded chalk hills, among railway trucks, and near a village with here and there an upper storey quite open like a loft. Snow. Gradually flatter and poplars regular as telegraph poles, orchards, level crossings, children. Buchy at 10 a.m.—Y.M.C.A.—Leave train. Nearly lost train. Fine snowfall. Furzy cuttings. Mistletoe in field, poplars by Alaincourt. Amiens at 2 and train left a score of men behind for a time. Pale sky and crimson sun at sunset. Doullens at 8. Guns all the time. Night with Thorburn at Resthouse. Thorburn had been very worried on journey—by things like tunnels while shaving etc.—then by dirty stories after tea. A restless night.

6. Still very cold. Men had only just drawn rations at 10 when parade was. Much ice on road and pavement. Hanging about in cafés or cold Resthouse. Fine dusty cold day. 2.50 fr. breakfast; 6 fr. lunch. Horton's amusing jaunty talk full of old army proverbs and metaphors and 'I mean to say.' Letter to Helen. No letters received since Codford. Suddenly at 7.30 we have to shift to Mondicourt without guns—I go on in lorry and choose billets—all in half-ruined barns—barns and farms here are a quad, entered through high arch and self-complete. We got an elephant sergeants mess to sleep in. Bitter cold, this being highest in Northern France. Roads ice and frozen snow. Farmyards all frozen. Kaffirs digging.

7. Bright cold. Horton's way of suddenly saying 'I will arise and go to my Father and say "Form Fours".' Indoors mostly, talking silly, arranging

mess funds etc.—I being secretary—cooking our dinner. Battery on short route march. We are to move up very soon. A very merry evening.

8. Weather as befcre. Physical drill, a hasty Welsh Rabbit with honey, and then off in lorries through Alaincourt, Barly, Fosseux, to Berneville—men billet in huge barn of a big uneven farmyard surrounded by spread arched stone barns and buildings with old pump at one side, kitchen at upper end. We forage. Enemy plane like pale moth beautiful among shrapnel bursts. A fine ride over high open snowy country with some woods. Rigging up table in mess and borrowing crockery. The battery is to split for the present: Rubin has taken guns to Saulty. We are for Dainville. A scramble dinner of half cold stuff, mostly standing. Taylor makes a table and says 'Very good, Sir' and 'It's the same for all. You gentlemen have to put up with same as us'. Bed early. Rubin returns late. Heavy firing at night. Restless.

9. Bright bitter cold. Rubin and Smith move off to join 146. Heavy firing near. Afternoon marched through Warlus to Dainville, billets on Arras road, with shell holes behind. Bitter cold. Tea with 146. Beds in the mess for night. (Remember Berneville courtyard, with ruined pigeon house by well and church behind and what was manor house). Graveyard for 3 'Mort pour la patrie' below our billet. A wonderful night of all the stars and low full moon. Officers of trench mortar battery detained here dine with us on bully, cheese and white wine.

10. Slept warm. Making latrines. With Debenham of 146 to see O.P.s [Observation Posts] and what was visible from them—through Achicourt and over railway towards Beaurains. One dead man under railway bridge. Maison brulé[e] dangerous. Map, field glass and compass over snowy broken land with posts and wires and dead trees. No infantry visible in our lines or Germans, except those we passed in trenches—Somersets and Cornwalls. Cloudy night and light wind but no thaw yet.

11. Milder and misty first—sun warm at noon. Maps in morning. After-noon with digging party at our position by Faubourg d'Amiens at southern edge of Arras in an orchard. After tea paid the battery for first time in France. Tested compass bearings by map. Cold. Rubin influenza. Thorburn to Arras. No letters yet. Censoring as usual. Gramophone playing 'Wait till I am as old as father' and 'Where does daddy go when he goes out?' 9 p.m. Great cannonade thudding and flashing quite con-tinuously away South in Ancre.

12. Disappointed in not going again on trench Reconnaissance. Maps in morning. Working party at gun position in afternoons. Got a chill and was very weary. Thorburn and Rubin have colds. Evening as usual

censoring men's letters. Halfbattery moves to Faubourg d'Amiens—
Thorburn there too, thank God. Smith back from Saulty—no news of
our letters or lorries. Not much firing near us today, but 146 lost a man
killed and one wounded. Gramophone plays the rotten things and then
Gounod's 'Ave Maria' and 'Dormezvous' which makes us rather silent
after smut.

13. Awoke tired and cold though it is thawing and cloudy with a breeze.
No work this morning, but I pore over map and think how I may enjoy
doing it when this is all over, which is not a good feeling, I suspect.
Taylor says (as he makes my bed and as usual asks if he does it right):
'I am not proud, but I likes to be comfortable. I have been domesticated
since I joined the Army.' Nothing to do all morning, afternoon at our
position—hare, partridges and wild duck in field S.E. of guns. I feel the
cold—the morning sun turns to a damp thaw wind. Letters home to
Father, Mother and Eleanor. Some grass showing green through melting
snow. Thorburn worries because he can't laugh at silly low talk. Evening
censoring letters and reading Sonnets; others writing—when I began to
talk to Rubin, the Captain said 'You get on with your Sonnets' and then
all was silent. Awful fug.

14. A bad night but feeling better. All day with Horton, and then Horton
and Smith, examining O.P.s above Agny and Wailly, and then between
Achicourt and Beaurains. Fine sunny day—snow melting. Black-headed
buntings talk, rooks caw, lovely white puffs of shrapnel round planes high
up. Right Section does aeroplane shoot in afternoon. Dead campion
umbels, and grass rustling on my helmet through trenches. Pretty little
copse in deep hollow high up between Ficheux and Dainville, where guns
look over to Berneville and Warlus.

15. With Captain observing for a BT. [Battery Training] shoot on
Ficheux Mill and edge of Blairville Wood. Fine sun but cold in trench.
With working party in afternoon. Letters arrived at 6. We sorted them
and then spent an hour silently reading. 750 letters for men; 17 for me—
from Helen, the children, Father, Mother, Eleanor, Freeman, Mrs.
Freeman, Guthrie, Vernon and Haines. Evening, reading and writing
letters. A quiet evening indoors and out. Taylor says as he mends the
fire, 'Well, we have to put up with many discomforts. We are all alike,
Sir, all human.' A still starry night with only machine guns and rifles.
Slept badly again, and then suddenly with no notice got up from breakfast
on the

16th to do fire control on aeroplane shoot (only 10 rounds, observation
being bad). Dull day. Left Thorburn on guns at 11.30. Bad temper. After-

noon up to O.P., but too hazy to observe. A mad Captain with several men driving partridges over the open and whistling and crying 'Mark over'. Kestrels in pairs. Four or five planes hovering and wheeling as kestrels used to over Mutton and Ludcombe. Women hanging clothes to dry on barbed entanglement across the road. Rain at last at 4.15. This morning the old Frenchman living in this ruin burst into our room while we were dressing to complain of our dirt and depredation, and when Rubin was rude in English said he was a Frenchman and had been an officer. Nobody felt the slightest sympathy with his ravings, more than with the old white horse who works a mill walking up and up treadmill.

17. A dull muddy day. No observation, no shooting. On guns all day and in dug-out, writing up our fighting book. Another letter from home. Could only just see A.P. [(First) Aid Post]. Kit arrived late last night. I slept badly, coughing. Very mild and the roads chalk and water, Grandes Graves 2.50 a bottle. Thorburn asks where he shall put the letters he has censored—decides on the crowded table—then I have to tell him the mantelpiece is the obvious place.

18. Another dull day down in 146 Dug-out. Afternoon to Arras—Town Hall like Carreg Cennin. Beautiful small white square empty. Top storey of high house ruined cloth armchair and a garment across it left as fly shell arrived. Car to Mendicourt and back by light of star shells. Shopping at Bellevue B.E.F. canteen. Returned to find I am to go as Orderly Officer to Group 35 H.A. [Heavy Artillery] in Arras tomorrow.

19. To Arras and began showing sectors and arcs on 1/10000 maps. Field Cashier's, waiting in long queue of officers to cash cheques etc. Learning office work. Place Victor Hugo white houses and shutters and sharpened fuller and dome in middle. Beautiful. In class it was like Bath—retired people, schools, priests. Gardens, courtyards, open spaces with trees. I still funk the telephone and did not use it once today. Sentries challenge in street and answer 'Sussex' etc.

20. Rain. To Fosseux in the car for cash and gas helmets. Rain and mud and troops and Hun prisoners and turbaned Indians at a barn door holding a sheep by a rope round its neck, all still and silent. Afternoon through Fosseux again with Col. Witchall to Mondicourt in rain and mud and back in darkness along main Arras Road—could usually only see 2 or 3 of the roadside trees except when we ran into the blaze of 18-pounder battery by roadside. Blast of 18-pounders near the billet blows mortar from ruins against our window linen. Called at 244 for letters—none. C/O [Commanding Officer (Colonel Witchall)] and Berrington and Cassels as before sat up till 12.30 and I could not get my bed before

21. Clearer and no rain. Checking inventory of new billet in fine modern house at corner of Rue de l'Abbé Hallain and Boulevard Vauban. Big vacant house, red brick and shutters, oak floors, panelling and pictured ceilings and mirrors—a few beds, chairs and tables left. A small backyard with a few trees and grass. We supplant Cameronians. One ruined house has still an engraved 1850 portrait hanging on wall high up, without glass broken. Rubin brought in letters from Helen and Eleanor. Hung on at old billet till telephone connection was made at new. It being very cold, we got to bed at 11.30.

22. Cold and wet. Fuel damp. Office work and maps. Court on Inquiry on gassing of 4 men. Am I to stay on here and do nothing but have cold feet and ask Cassels What is to be done? No thrushes yet, but a chaffinch says 'Chink' in the chestnut in our garden. Pipits sing up at Daneville, where I have come to see 244, but they are all out—they came in, all but O/C, and we had tea, and Rubin drove me back. Letter from Father. Evening in Mess with Wallace as guest. Cold and still: no artillery all day. At night I quite thought someone was knocking excitedly at one of the doors, when it was really machine guns. Troops going out to trenches singing and whistling 'It's nice to get up in the morning' or a thing with part of 'The Minstrel Boy' tune in it.

23. Chaffinch sang once. Another dull cold day. Inspected stables, checked inventory of new billet for men in Rue Jeanne d'Arc, went with Colonel round 244, 141 and 234 positions and O.P. in Achicourt. After-noon maps. Partridges twanging in fields. Flooded fields by stream between the 2 sides of Achicourt. Ruined churches, churchyard and rail-way. Sordid ruin of Estaminet with carpenter's shop over it in Rue Jeanne d'Arc—wet, mortar, litter, almanacs, bottles, broken glass, damp beds, dirty paper, knife, crucifix, statuette, old chairs. Our cat moves with the Group wherever it goes, but inspects new house inside and out, windows, fireplace etc. Paid the Pool gunners (scrapings from several batteries doing odd jobs here). 2 owls in garden at 6. The shelling must have slaughtered many jackdaws but has made home for many more. Finished Frost's 'Mountain Interval'. Wrote to Frost. A quiet still evening. Rubin brought over letters from Helen and Oscar.

24. Why do Huns not retaliate on Arras guns? Some day this will be one of the hottest places this side of Hell, if it is this side. Nothing to do here today. Clearer, but still dull and cold with more breeze. Gas Alert off. Wrote to Father. Lushington calls and goes out with Colonel W—. Dined with 244 and Major Berrington and Capt. Angus—a dull long meal with maraschino chocolates at end. Benedictine, whisky and coffee, after soup, hors d'oeuvres, tinned turkey, roast mutton, Christmas pudding, apricots

and cream. Gramophone but no fun. Walked back to Arras in dark with Thorburn, challenged by *only 2 sentries* who were content with 'Friend' though they could not see a yard among the ruins. Owls on Daneville Road. Machine guns and hanging lights above No Man's Land. Cassells and Colonel alone up when I returned at 11. New moon—*last* as I walked from Hatch to Codford.

25. A dull morning turns sunny and warm. Chaffinches and partridges, moles working on surface. Beautiful 18th century citadel with church ruined in middle of great barrack square. Huge bastions with sycamores in moat and tangled grass. Walked over citadel to new position with Colonel. Talked to Horton in our orchard. Wrote to Oscar. Artillery lively in the clear sunny noon. I got hot and spring-languid walking up at 4.30 to 244. Gramophone here played 'Anitra's Dance', 'Death of Troll' etc. and 'Allanwater'. Does a mole ever get hit by a shell?

26. A clear morning. 8.15-9.30 a.m. incessant field-gun firing—raid—German prisoners back at 10.15. Sunshine in white ruins and white squares with Scots standing about. A few shells arrive in Arras, but nobody looked as if anything were happening. While our guns were firing we could not hear one another speak. Afternoon to Achicourt to see if a gun position was visible to Huns. Shells and machine gun bullets came over. An 18-pounder on a fire point fired when I was 3 yards off (in front). Fitting aeroplane photos together. Paid out. A sunny day but cold in this house. Wrote to G. Bottomley. Gramophone. Talk with Berrington and Colonel.

27. Fine but chilly. 2 English planes fell, one on fire, as I walked up to 244 in afternoon: machine gun bullets cut telephone wire close by. Letters from Helen and Irene. Nothing to do but go and see about a billet of 244's collared by another Battery. Tea at 244 after seeing 2 of our planes down, one on fire with both burnt to death after alighting. Letters from Helen, Irene and Eleanor.

28. 244 to go into position. Out identifying gun positions. Up to 244 to pack for a change of billet. Tea with Rubin, Thorburn, Lushington and Horton. Letter from Helen, parcel from Mother. Shelling town at night. Walk out to Daneville by citadel and marsh—moorhens in clear chalk stream by incinerator; blackbirds too, but no song except hedge-sparrow. Evening, ruin with Colonel and Cassells.

## MARCH

1. Sunny and breezy. Wrote to Helen, Mother, Eleanor and Ellis. Indoors all morning doing nothing. Mostly a quiet morning. Out with Berrington

round the marsh towards 244 who were doing their 1st shoot. Enemy planes over. 2 rounds across 244 position on to Doullens Road. Great deal of anti-aircraft shells singing by. Sat down on hill above 244 and watched German lines and Beaurains ghastly trees and ruins above Achicourt church tower. A bullet passes. Quite warm to sit down for quarter hour. Evening in mess. Colonel talks of the General (Poole) who was all for 'Fire, fire, fire! Loose her off! Deliver the goods! Annoy the Hun.' with artillery. Shelling heavy from about 5 a.m. I only dressed because I thought it would be better to have my clothes on. In any case I had to be up at 6 to go to Achicourt. A very misty still morning: could see nothing from bedroom except the trees and the stone dog—our artillery really made most of the noise, and I being just wakened and also inexperienced mistook it.

2. Up at 5.30 and went out to Achicourt Chateau to see 141's gun into its forward position. A misty frosty morning luckily and no plane could observe. Afternoon to Faubourg Ronville, its whistling deserted ruined streets. deserted roadway, pavement with single files of men. Cellars as dugouts, trenches behind and across road. Dead dry calf in stable. Rubble, rubbish, filth and old plush chair. Perfect view of No Man's Land winding level at foot of Hun slope, and Beaurains above to one side and woods just behind crest on other side (M.B.110) [a map reference (?Bench Mark)]. With Horton and Lushington to see 3 O.P.s there:—Letters from Helen, Mother, Eleanor and J. Freeman.

3.[6] No post. Morning dull spent in office. But afternoon with Colonel to Achicourt to see O.P.s and then to new battery positions. A chilly day not good for observing. Court of Inquiry on a man burnt with petrol— Lushington presiding and afterwards I went back with him to 244's new billet and saw my new quarters to be. Wrote to Mother and Helen.

4. Cold but bright clear and breezy. Nothing to do all morning but trace a map and its contours. Colonel and I went down to 244 before lunch to see the shell holes of last night and this morning. Hun planes over. More shells came in the afternoon. The fire is warm but the room cold. Tea with Lushington and Thorburn. Shelling at 5.30—I don't like it. I wonder where I shall be hit as in bed I wonder if it is better to be on the window or outer side of room or on the chimney on inner side, whether better to be upstairs where you may fall or on the ground floor where you may be worse crushed. Birthday parcels from home.

5. Out early to see a raid by VI Corps [the main Army Command Group in this area], but snow hid most but singing of Field shells and snuffling

[6] Thomas's thirty-ninth birthday.

of 6".—Ronville's desolate streets. To 244's orchard which has had numerous 4.2 shells over, meant for the road. Wrote to Helen, Mervyn and Bronwen. Afternoon indoors paying etc. After tea to 244 to dine, not very happy with Lushington, Horton and Smith. They have the wind up because of the shells (which may have been meant for the road behind). Letters from de la Mare, Helen, Bronwen and de la Mare. A beautiful clear moonlit night after a beautiful high blue day with combed white clouds.

6. Bright and clear early and all day and warm at 1. Walked over to 244's position with Colonel and then up to 234 beyond Daneville station, and listened to larks and watched aeroplane fights. 2 planes down, one in flames, a Hun. Sometimes 10 of our planes together very high. Shells into Arras in afternoon.

7. A cold raw dull day with nothing to do except walk round to 244 to get a pair of socks. The wind made a noise in the house and trees and a dozen black crumpled sycamore leaves dance round and round on terrace. Wrote to Pearce and Irene. Rather a cold and depressed, solitary.

8. Snow blizzard—fine snow and fierce wind—to Achicourt O.P. but suddenly a blue sky and soft white cloud through the last of the snow— with Colonel and Berrington. Returned to hear that the Group has to leave this billet. I liked the walk. Indoors afternoon fitting together aeroplane trench photographs. Letters from Helen, Eleanor, Oscar and Frost (saying he had got an American publisher for my verses). A still quiet night up to 11 with just one round fired to show we have not left Arras. Up till 1 for a despatch from Corps. Colonel snotted interpreter.

9. Snow and very cold indoors doing nothing but look at a sandbag O.P. My last day at the Group. Weir of 2/1 Lowland takes my place. I return to 244—Lushington, Horton and Rubin. I am fed up with sitting on my arse doing nothing that anybody couldn't do better. Wrote to de la Mare, Frost and Eleanor.

10. Up at 5.45 for a raid, but nothing doing. A misty mild morning clearing slightly to a white sky. 10 rounds gunfire C-B [?Command Battery]. Snowdrops at foot of peartrees by Decanville Railway. R.F.C. [Royal (?) Flying Corps] wireless man reading 'Hiawatha'. 3 shoots of 10 rounds gunfire suddenly at N.F. targets [no fixed targets] unobserved. Men mending a caved-in dugout in the dark. Parcel from Janet Hooton.

11. Out at 8.30 to Ronville O.P. and studied the ground from Beaurains N. Larks singing over No Man's Land—trench mortars. We were bombarding their front line: they were shooting at Arras. R.F.A. [Royal

Field Artillery] officer with me who was quite concerned till he spotted a certain familiar Hun sentry in front line. A clear, cloudy day, mild and breezy. 8th shell carrying into Arras. Later Ronville heavily shelled and we retired to dugout. At 6.15 all quiet and heard blackbirds chinking. Scene peaceful, desolate like Dunwich moors except sprinkling of white chalk on the rough brown ground. Lines broken and linesmen out from 2.30 to 7 p.m. A little raid in the night . . .,

12. . . . then a beautiful moist clear limpid early morning till the Raid at 7 and the retaliation on Ronville at 7.30–8.45 with 77 cm. 25 to the minute. Then back through 6 ins. of chalk mud in trenches along battered Ronville Street. Rooks in tall trees on N. side of Arras—they and their nests and the trees black against the soft clouded sky. W. wind and mild but no rain yet (11 a.m.). Letters, mess accounts, maps. Afternoon at maps and with Horton at battery. Evening of partridges calling and pip-squeaks coming over behind.

13. Blackbird trying to sing early in dull marsh. A dull cold day. One N.F. shoot at nightfall. I was in position all day. Letters from Eleanor, Mother and Ellis: wrote to Bronwen, Mother and Eleanor.

14. Ronville O.P. Looking out towards No Man's Land what I thought first was a piece of burnt paper or something turned out to be a bat shaken at last by shells from one of the last sheds in Ronville. A dull cold morning, with some shelling of Arras and St. Sauveur and just 3 for us. Talking to Birt and Randall about Glostershire and Wiltshire, particularly Pains-wick and Marlborough. A still evening—blackbirds singing far off—a spatter of our machine guns—the spit of one enemy bullet—a little rain—no wind—only far-off artillery.

15. Huns strafe I sector at 5.30. We reply and they retaliate on Arras and Ronville. Only tired 77s reach OP. A sunny breezy morning. Tried to climb Arras chimney to observe, but funked. 4 shells nearly got me while I was going and coming. A rotten day. No letters for 5 days.

16. Larks and great tits. Ploughing field next to orchard in mist—horses and man go right up to crest in view of Hun at Beaurains. Cold and dull. Letters to Helen and Janet. In the battery for the day. Fired 100 rounds from 12–1.30. Sun shining but misty still. Letter from Bronwen. The first thrush I have heard in France sang as I returned to Mess at 6 p.m. Parcel from Mother—my old Artist boots. Wrote to Hodson. A horrible night of bombardment, and the only time I slept I dreamt I was at home and couldn't stay to tea . . .

17. . . . Then a most glorious bright high clear morning. But even Horton, disturbed by 60-pounders behind his dugout, came in to breakfast saying:

'I am not going to stay in this —— army; on the day peace is declared I am out of it like a —— rabbit'. A beautiful day, sunny with pale cloudless sky and W. wind, but cold in O.P. Clear nightfall with curled, cinereous cloud and then a cloudless night with pale stains in sky over where Bosh is burning a village or something. Quiet till 3: then a Hun raid and our artillery over us to meet it: their shells into St. Sauveur, Ronville and Arras. Sound of fan in underground cave.

18. Beautiful clear cloudless morning and no firing between daybreak and 8. Drew another panorama at 7. Linnets and chaffinches sing in waste trenched ground with trees and water tanks between us and Arras. Magpies over No Man's Land in pairs. The old green (grey) track crossing No Man's Land—once a country way to Arras. The water green and clear (like Silent Pool) of the Moat of the Citadel with skeletons of whole trees lying there. Afternoon washing and reading letters from Helen and Eleanor. I did 2 shoots. News came that we are in Beaurains and near Mercatel. Letters to Helen and Eleanor. The pigeons are about in the streets of this Faubourg more than ever and I could hear a lark till the Archies drowned it. Fired 600 rounds and got tired eyes and ears. Then early to bed and up at 4 to go to O.P. on

19. Nothing to do all day at Ronville but look at quiet No Man's Land and trenches with engineers beginning to straighten road up. Back to sleep at billet, but preferred to return to O.P. as I've to go to the front trench O.P. at 4 on the

20th. Stiff deep mud all the way up and shelled as we started. Telegraph Hill as quiet as if only rabbits lived there. I took revolver and left this diary behind in case. For it is very exposed and only a few Cornwalls and MGC [Machine Gun Corps] about. But Hun shelled chiefly over our heads into Beaurains all night—like starlings returning 20 or 30 a minute. Horrible flap of 5·9 a little along the trench. Rain and mud and I've to stay till I am relieved tomorrow. Had not brought warm clothes or enough food and had no shelter, nor had telephonists. Shelled all night. But the M.G.C. boy gave me tea. I've no bed. I leant against wall of trench. I got up and looked over. I stamped up and down. I tried to see patrol out. Very light—the only sign of Hun on Telegraph Hill, though 2 appeared and were sniped at. A terribly long night and cold. Not relieved till 8. Telephonists out repairing line since 4 on the morning of the

21st. At last 260 relieved us. Great pleasure to be going back to sleep and rest. No Man's Land like Goodwood Racecourse with engineers swarming over it and making a road between shell holes full of blood-stained water and beer bottles among barbed wire. Larks singing as they did when we went up in dark and were shelled. Now I hardly felt as if a shell could hurt, though several were thrown about near working parties. Found letters from Helen, Eleanor and Julian. Had lunch, went to bed at 2 intending to get up to tea, but slept till 6.30 on the . . .

22nd. (Beautiful was Arras yesterday coming down from Beaurains and seeing Town Hall ruin white in sun like a thick smoke beginning to curl. Sprinkle of snow today in sun.) A cold bright day with snow early. We fired twice. I on duty at Battery. Letters to Helen and home and Gordon and Deacon. Partridges twanging in open fields. Not much shooting to do. Several windy snow showers half-hail and then sun. Talk with Thorburn about his fate if he loses his commission. Gramophone plays Ambrose Thomas's 'Mignon' gavotte (by Raymond Jeremy's Philharmonic Quartette), 'D'ye ken John Peel', Chopin's 'Berceuse', Tchaikovsky's 'Fantasia Italiana'.

23. Frosty clear. Ploughs going up over crest towards Beaurains. Rubin back from F.O.P. [Forward Observation Post (in No Man's Land)] believes in God and tackles me about atheism—thinks marvellous escapes are ordained. But I say so are the marvellous escapes of certain telegraph posts, houses, etc. Sunny and cold—motored to Avesnes and Fosseux to buy luxuries and get letters. Crowded bad roads through beautiful hedgeless rolling chalk country with rows of trees, some along roads following curving ridges—villages on crests with church spires and trees. Troops, children holding hands, and darkskinned women, mud walled ruined barns. Parcels from Mother and Helen, letters from Mother and J. Freeman.

24. Out early to Beaurains. The chill clear air pains my skin while it delights my mind—both walking and in car. Only tombstones recognisable in Beaurains and that little conical summer house among trees. Sat all day in copse in old chalk pit between Agny and Achicourt which is perhaps to be our new position. Warm in the sun, but no thrushes in all those ash, hazel and dogwood. Parcels from Mrs. Freeman and Eleanor. Letters to Helen, Mrs. Freeman and Mother.

25. Up at 5 and to O.P. beyond Beaurains with Thorburn and stood all day in trench behind hedge till head ached with staring at Wancourt and Neuville Vitasse and the ground between and beyond. A cold but sunny day. Many R.F.A. and infantry used the O.P. We were discovered and the O.P. 20 yards away had a shell on to it, and we had several over our shoulders. Larks singing. Drawing panoramas. Left Thorburn there at 6 p.m. tired enough. Letters from Bronwen, [R. C.] Trevelyan and Guthrie.

26. Preparing reports and panoramas for 35 H.A.G. [Heavy Artillery Group]. Rainy and dull. Letter to Bronwen. Packing up for move to the chalk pit. Up late in emptied billet waiting for ASC [Army Service Corps] lorries to come up. Off at last on foot to the Achicourt billet at 1, in white cordite flashes in dark roads.

27. Rain and sleet and sun, getting guns camouflaged, stealing a Decan-ville truck, laying out nightlines. Letters from Hodson, Eleanor and Sgt. Pellissier. Still that aching below the nape of my neck since my last O.P. day. Sat till 11 writing letters. As I was falling asleep great blasts shook the house and windows, whether from our own firing or enemy bursts near, I could not tell in my drowse, but I did not doubt my heart thumped so that if they had come closer together it might have stopped. Rubin and Smith dead tired after being up all the night before. Letters to Helen and Eleanor.

28. Frosty and clear and some blackbirds singing at Agny Chateau in the quiet of exhausted battery, everyone just having breakfast at 9.30: all very still and clear: but these mornings always very misleading and disappearing so that one might almost think afterwards they were illusive. Planes humming. In high white cloud aeroplanes leave tracks curving like rough wheel tracks in snow—I had a dream this morning that I have forgot but Mother was in distress. All day loading shells from old position —sat doing nothing till I got damned philosophical and sad. Thorburn dreamt 2 nights ago that a maid was counting forks and spoons and he asked her 'Must an officer be present.' Letter to Helen. Tired still.

29. Wet again. Getting refuge trenches dug for detachments. Marking crests on map. How beautiful, like a great crystal sparkling and spangling, the light reflected from some glass which is visible at certain places and times through a hole in cathedral wall, ruined cathedral.

30. Bright early, then rain. New zero line, planting pickets. Arranging for material for new O.P. dugout—old one fell in yesterday. Clear and bright and still from 6 p.m. on. Air full of planes and sound of whistles against Hun planes. Blackbirds singing and then chuckling as they go to roost. Two shells falling near Agny Chateau scatter them. Letters from Helen and Mother and parcels from Mother and Eleanor. Too late to bed and had no sleep at all, for the firing, chiefly 60-pounders of our own. Shakespeare's plays for 10 minutes before sleep.

31. Up at 5 worn out and wretched. 5.9s flopping on Achicourt while I dressed. Up to Beaurains. There is a chalk-stone cellar with a dripping Bosh dug-out far under and by the last layer of stones is the lilac bush, rather short. Nearby a graveyard for the 'tapferer franzos soldat' with

crosses and Hun names. Blackbirds in the clear cold bright morning early in black Beaurains. Sparrows in the elder of the hedge I observe through —a cherry tree just this side of hedge makes projection in trench with its roots. Beautiful clear evening everything dark and soft round Neuville Vitasse, after the rainbow there and the last shower. Night in lilac-bush cellar of stone like Berryfield. Letter to Helen. Machine gun bullets snaking along—hissing like little wormy serpents.

## APRIL

1. among the ragged and craggy gables of Beaurains—a beautiful serene clear morning with larks at 5.15 and blackbirds at 6 till it snowed or rained at 8. All day sat writing letters to Helen, Father and Mother by the fire and censoring men's letters etc., an idle day—I could not sleep till I went to bed at 10. Letters from Helen, Baba and Deacon. A fine bright day with showers.

2. Letter to H. K. Vernon. Another frosty clear windy morning. Some sun and I enjoyed filling sandbags for dug out we are to have in battery for the battle. But snow later after we had fired 100 rounds blind. Snow half melting as it falls makes fearful slush. I up at battery alone till 9.30 p.m. Writing to Helen and Frost. Rubin and Smith sang duets from 'Bing Boys' till 11.

3. Snow just frozen—strong S.E. wind. Feet wet by 8.15 a.m. Letters from Gordon and Freeman. The eve. Letters to Gordon, Freeman, Helen. A fine day later, filling sandbags. MACBETH.

4. Up at 4.30. Blackbirds sing at battery at 5.45—shooting at 6.30. A cloudy fresh morning. But showery cold muddy and slippery later. 600 rounds. Nothing in return yet. Tired by 9.15 p.m. Moved to dug-out in position. Letter from Helen. Artillery makes air flap all night long.

5. A dull morning turns misty with rain. Some 4·2s coming over at 10. Air flapping all night as with great sails in strong gusty wind (with artillery)—thick misty windless air. Sods on f/c's dugout begin to be fledged with fine green feathers of yarrow — yarrow. Sun and wind drying the mud. Firing all day, practising barrage etc. Beautiful pale hazy moonlight and the sag and flap of air. Letters to Mother and Helen. HAMLET.

6. A lazy morning, being a half day: warm and breezy, with sun and cloud but turned wet. Billets shelled by 4·2: 60-pounders hit. In car with Horton to Fosseux and Avesnes and met infantry with yellow patches behind marching soaked up to line—band and pipes at Wanquetin to greet them, playing 'They wind up the Watch on the Rhine' (as Horton calls it). After the shelling Horton remarks: 'The Bosh is a damned good

man, isn't he, a damned smart man, you must admit'. Roads worse than ever—no crust left on side roads. Letters from Helen, Mervyn, Mother, Eleanor.

7. Up at 6 to O.P. A cold bright day of continuous shelling N. Vitasse and Telegraph Hill. Infantry all over the place in open preparing Prussian Way with boards for wounded. Hardly any shells into Beaurains. Larks, partridges, hedgesparrows, magpies by O.P. A great burst in red brick building in N. Vitasse stood up like a birch tree or a fountain. Back at 7.30 in peace. Then at 8.30 a continuous roar of artillery.

8. A bright warm Easter day but Achicourt shelled at 12.39 and then at 2.15 so that we all retired to cellar. I had to go over to battery at 3 for a practice barrage, skirting the danger zone, but we were twice interrupted. A 5·9 fell 2 yards from me as I stood by the f/c post. One burst down the back of the office and a piece of dust scratched my neck. No firing from 2-4. Rubin left for a course.

On the last pages of diary are these notes:

The light of the new moon and every star

And no more singing for the bird . . .

I never understood quite what was meant by God

The morning chill and clear hurts my skin while it delights my mind.

Neuville in early morning with its flat straight crest with trees and houses [see Diary, April 1]—the beauty of this silent empty scene of no inhabitants and hid troops, but don't know why I could have cried and didn't.

Loose inside the diary, strangely creased by shell-blast like the diary, is a photograph of Helen and an army pass to Loughton/Lydd dated 3.12.16. Also a slip of paper with addresses of S. N. Jones of Newport, H. K. Vernon of Oxford, J. N. Benson of Upper Tooting, Lewis John of Upminster, his brother Julian Thomas in Tooting. On the reverse of this in pencil is written

Where any turn may lead to Heaven

Or any corner may hide Hell

Roads shining like river up hill after rain.[7]

---

[7] Cf. Poem 96, fourth and seventh stanzas.

# INDEX OF FIRST LINES

# INDEX OF FIRST LINES